T0109308

THE
SELF-DISCIPLINE
HANDBOOK

SIMPLE WAYS TO CULTIVATE SELF-DISCIPLINE,
BUILD CONFIDENCE, AND OBTAIN YOUR GOALS

NATALIE WISE

Skyhorse Publishing

Copyright © 2017 by Natalie Wise

All Rights Reserved. No part of this book may be reproduced in any manner without the express written consent of the publisher, except in the case of brief excerpts in critical reviews or articles. All inquiries should be addressed to Skyhorse Publishing, 307 West 36th Street, 11th Floor, New York, NY 10018.

Skyhorse Publishing books may be purchased in bulk at special discounts for sales promotion, corporate gifts, fund-raising, or educational purposes. Special editions can also be created to specifications. For details, contact the Special Sales Department, Skyhorse Publishing, 307 West 36th Street, 11th Floor, New York, NY 10018 or info@skyhorsepublishing.com.

www.skyhorsepublishing.com

10 9 8 7 6 5 4 3 2

Library of Congress Cataloging-in-Publication Data is available on file.

ISBN: 978-1-5107-2487-7
eBook ISBN: 978-1-5107-2488-4

Cover design by Jenny Zemanek
Cover photo by istockphoto

Printed in China

"I can do all things through Christ who strengthens me."
—Philippians 4:13

To the One who revives me each morning with new mercies, who fills my heart with grace when it is fainting, who takes my heavy burden and makes it light, who saw discipline through to the cross, and then to the crown . . . to you, Jesus, who makes self-discipline (the thing itself and the book) possible.

CONTENTS

INTRODUCTION

....

What *is* self-discipline? We all seem to know we need it. More of it. I don't know anyone who thinks they need *less* self-discipline. We know we need it, yet we all seem a bit foggy on the actual definition. Is it being on time to everything? Or early? Waking up at 5 a.m.? Doing everything everyone asks us to, on time, all the time? Does self-discipline run us ragged, chew us up, and spit us out eventually, or is it something deeper? Something more meaningful, perhaps. Something more nourishing. Something not-so-scary, not-so-distasteful.

Perhaps self-discipline, more than being something we lament needing more of, should be something we take joy in cultivating. Something that feeds us, rather than depletes us. Of course, we aren't always very good at taking care of ourselves, so it's no surprise we're still wondering how to get more of this elusive magic-sauce that is self-discipline.

Have no fear. This handbook delves into the art and science of self-discipline. What it is, how to get it, why we need it, how to keep it, and why we want it. It also covers the major stumbling blocks in our way, both internally and externally.

Self-discipline has many friends. It also has many foes, and I have made peace with the self-discipline devils. You can, too.

"Nothing is so fatiguing as the eternal hanging-on of an unfinished task." —William James

Who Am I to Write about Self-Discipline?

I'm no scientist, and I don't study the way our brains work and what makes us scientifically more likely to keep or not keep resolutions. But I've been practicing the art of self-discipline since I was very young. I started high school when I was twelve, not because I was particularly smart, but because I worked hard and was motivated. I enjoyed Latin class, took AP classes, did dual-enrollment, and graduated at fifteen with a year's worth of college credits alongside my diploma. I graduated college at age nineteen, before taking a few years off. On my twenty-first birthday I started a Master's program in Poetry at Dartmouth College and graduated when I was twenty-two. I've been published in the *New Yorker*, written several books, been featured on a television show, and worked with many influential people, and I'm not even thirty yet.

Does this make me special? Does this make me Superwoman? I don't think so, and neither should you. Did I work harder than your average teen? Absolutely. Did I also wear myself out and spend a few years completely crashing and burning? Yes, yes, I did that as well. See, I've done this self-discipline thing both ways. I've been on top of the world with green juices and aerobics before 5 a.m., and I've fallen into the self-discipline depression hole that is my bed for days on end. And I've learned a few things from both.

We will take a look at the science, because science has plenty of great things to say about how our brains work. But self-discipline also requires heart, spirit, and motivation, things science still doesn't have a great handle on. It takes a more creative approach to figure out what makes those things work, and they are crucial for positive self-discipline.

> *"Let us, then, be up and doing . . .*
> *Still achieving, still pursuing . . ."*
> *—Henry Wadsworth Longfellow*

WHAT IS SELF-DISCIPLINE?

••••••••••••••••••

The two words themselves have a rather unpleasant meaning at first glance, implying that we "punish ourselves." But the term is more nuanced.

Oxford dictionaries says self-discipline is "the ability to control one's feelings and overcome one's weaknesses; the ability to pursue what one thinks is right despite temptations to abandon it."[1] A verb. An action, an exchange of energy.

To do what we think is *right*, despite **temptations** to **abandon** it. Wow, that means a lot more than "punish ourselves," don't you think? It means passion and purpose, because we are doing what we think is right. Not what we think is our duty. Not what we, or others, have forced on us. It is a strongheart thing, a gritted-teeth thing. Temptations. Ahh, that major foe. Temptation is all around, literally. Temptation is also within us, that sly little inner self that says, "Do it tomorrow, really, you'll be fine."

Does this mean getting up at 5 a.m. every morning? Maybe. Does this mean knowing you need a break from getting

---

1   *Oxford Dictionaries, s.v.* "self-discipline." https://en.oxforddictionaries. com/definition/us/self-discipline.

up at 5 a.m. so you don't burn out? Maybe. Keep in mind that self-discipline is not self-flagellation. Self-discipline is useful, a tool. Self-flagellation is negative, a punishment.

Forgoing self-discipline, or being very sloppy in our execution, therefore equates to abandoning what we think is *right*. That alone gives me motivation. That makes me want to take heart, to pick up the slack in my life and to tell those weaknesses of mine, "Buck up. We got this."

So I say to you, too: Buck up. You got this. You're obviously motivated to get a handle on self-discipline, because otherwise this book wouldn't be in your hands right now. Way to go! This book is a guidebook, because you are the only one who knows yourself. Use these tools to your best advantage. I've made it easy for you by including spaces to journal, draw, and list. The act of writing things down and getting them out of your head is powerful. Actually journal in the spots provided. Add your own tips and tricks. Highlight, underline, star, and annotate. I'm cheering you on. Let's get started!

THE BEGINNINGS OF SELF-DISCIPLINE

....

Self-discipline is one of those scientific anomalies that keeps scientists scratching their heads through the decades. The explanations for the hows and whys of self-discipline seem just as elusive in the scientific world as they are in real life. There are just so many variables.

The relatively simple Energy Model of Self-Control asserts that the brain has a finite amount of energy at any given time, and that it can be self-controlled *if* there is enough energy left. Each act of self-discipline depletes energy, so we are successively less likely to be strong. Once it's used up, it's all about the donuts, the couch, and the Netflix instead of the veggies, the gym, and the protein smoothie. This model leaves a major question—namely, how can we refuel the brain's energy? It appears the brain is refueled by simple carbohydrates like sugar. The old phrase of snacks being "brain food" wasn't too far off. Feeling weak? Pop a pack of M&Ms and all is well? Seems too good to be true, and, if you're trying to lose weight, counterproductive. But really what you're looking for is to increase blood glucose levels, so even sucking on a hard candy or swishing some sugar water around in your mouth can actually help. I'd suggest a few berries, though, as fruits are also simple carbohydrates and much more useful to the self-discipline agenda.[2]

But science also says our self-discipline is a muscle we can strengthen by using. Sugar helps power the muscle, but the stronger the muscle is, the more it can do. This is good news, because it means that when we work on improving our inner selves, the work can stick. We do get stronger. It doesn't happen overnight, but neither does body-building. We have to work our way up to the power-lifting of self-discipline. The magic formula, then, according to science: make small choices well, fuel your body correctly and consistently, and work on making more and bigger self-discipline choices.

Make Small Choices Well: The small choices in our lives accumulate to have a big impact. One small choice provides the momentum we need and the little boost of self-confidence to set us up for bigger and more demanding choices. Small choices might include drinking a glass of water with breakfast every day, flossing every night, or making one cold call a day to potential clients. Small positive choices set us up for success.

Fuel Your Body Correctly: Fueling your body well and avoiding blood glucose highs and lows is important for making good choices. Keep a mix of protein and carbohydrate/simple sugar snacks in your desk or car. When you feel your willpower

---

2 Association for Psychological Science, "Where Does Self-Discipline Come From?" http://www.psychologicalscience.org/news/full-frontal-psychology/where-does-self-discipline-come-from.html.

waning, grab a handful of raisins and almonds to keep you going. Experiment. See if you feel the difference in decision-making abilities with good, real-food simple sugars versus nothing at all, or poor food choices. Taking a minute to notice the positive effects makes it easier to stick with healthy snacking.

Add More Weight: Adding more self-discipline weight means adding more and/or bigger decisions. You'll want to do this gradually. Don't suddenly decide to conquer the world before 9 a.m., cycle 30 miles, be fully available emotionally for everyone in your life, day and night, and to cure cancer on the side. This is only setting yourself up for failure. Add more weight slowly, but consistently. Give yourself a solid week or two to really settle into each additional self-discipline task before adding another.

It would seem all we need to do is feed our bodies well to make good decisions. This is partly true, but it isn't the whole truth. Because science, try as it might, can't look at the inner self, the subconscious, the unconscious.

Define Success: Success is a nebulous thing; it doesn't fit neatly into any one box, and it's tough to describe exactly what it looks like. But defining benchmarks for success will give you direction and keep you motivated.

I am not talking about goal setting yet. Goal setting is *how* you get to success. Success is the end result. Goal setting is a valuable tool to meeting success, but we have to define success before we can set goals.

My success is not your success. This is a good thing, and it's what makes the world go 'round, but it also makes defining our own version of success a bit more difficult. It can take a little soul-searching. Success at work is different from personal relationship success. Success for you *now* might look different from what it has in the past, or from what your family thinks it should look like. Others might think your definition of success isn't "right," but it's really not their concern. Success is your own measure. Take hold of that truth. Success belongs to you and you alone. If someone else tries to define your success, you get to choose how to handle that. If you like their idea, incorporate it into your own. If you don't, it's no skin off your back because you haven't lost anything.

How do we define our own personal success markers? It boils down to this: what makes us feel that we've done our very best? This means that success is actually fluid. The definition of success, the target of success, is constantly changing. Don't freak out as we begin our self-discipline journey with this revelation. It is actually a good thing. We want success to be fluid. Life is fluid, and self-discipline is fluid, so it makes sense that the result would be, too. Sometimes the main goal stays the same, "Run a successful business of my own," while the details of the success change. Maybe you thought you wanted to own a multinational, thousands-of-employees business. That was your initial idea of a successful business. But life happens, and you realize that, actually, you're quite content with a regional business that has hundreds of employees and none of the stress of international business. The result didn't change, but the details did. This is how success is meant to work.

So we don't need to be so specific about our success, which takes a lot of the pressure off. Setting goals is good, yes.

And having a list of things to accomplish is great, too. But we needn't become so obsessed with a particular path to success that we forget the destination. Success at being healthy might come from eating better, exercising more, sleeping more, or any number of other things. And those things might change over time, just as your idea of what "healthy" means to you might evolve over time. Success in personal relationships might come from setting aside more time to nurture relationships at one point in your life, or setting more boundaries at another point.

Understand Your Values: Success is directly related to your values. Do you know what your values are? Values can be things like financial security, being close to family, health, independence, time freedom, and just about anything else in life that you put above other things. You get to decide what you value most. It's not inherently wrong to value financial security more than your family members do, for example. Your values will define your choices and your path, which may very well be different from someone else's choices and path—even someone you respect.

Make a list of the things that are important to you. Dig deep and be honest with yourself, remembering that no value is inherently bad. Also keep in mind that values change as we grow and mature, so what you used to value may not still hold true. Then, order them from most important to least important. Pick the top three to focus on. Any more than three and we tend to get overwhelmed. These will be your guiding principles in everything you do. Values inform self-discipline.

MY VALUES

_____

_____

_____

_____

_____

_____

_____

_____

_____

_____

_____

_____

_____

_____

_____

_____

_____

_____

_____

_____

_____

_____

_____

_____

Values keep you going when the going gets tough. Values help you pull from deep reserves of strength you didn't know you had, because you want to, you have to, you can, and you will for the things you value.

We do not go above and beyond for things we don't care about. And I don't believe that's the point of self-discipline. Self-discipline is designed to help you improve, and why improve the things you don't care about? No, we want to be disciplined in our lives so we can honor our values and create our own personal definition of success that we can meet with contentment.

Duty. See, duty's the thing that most people get confused with self-discipline. A sense of duty is hard-wired into some of us, and we will do almost anything if we feel we must. Now, there are some things we must do out of responsibility, such as attending work meetings or showing up when you're the leader of a group. Responsibility is different—you've signed on because you want to, because this task gives you something (money, respect, influence, the chance to help others). You've already made a value-based choice, and responsibility is following through with it.

And of course, there is actual guilt, when you mess up and you feel guilty for not coming through. But there is fear-guilt as well, which is less than virtuous. The reason we do things out of duty is that we may feel guilty if we don't. And what is this kind of guilt? Fear-guilt. Fear-guilt is not true; it is based on fear that someone else will think we are "less than." And you are not "less than," no matter what anyone says. You will not be "less than" if you don't go to every board meeting of the board you're on. You will not be "less than" if you don't go to church every Sunday, or "less than" if you don't show up to preschool drop-off in the latest fashions. Duty is a liar. Do things out of value and you will find your self-discipline skyrockets.

Now, you can do things out of value that are slightly dutiful, as well. For instance, you might not want to go to your spouse's work party. It doesn't add value to your life. But it adds value to your spouse's life to have you there. And one of your values is family. So this becomes something you are pleased to do to add value to your spouse and your relationship, rather than a task you must complete out of duty and drudgery. And trust me, doing something for a spouse of out duty and drudgery won't go over very well. They can sniff that out a mile away. Change your mindset and see how it changes the outcome.

Chart a Roadmap: Once you've defined your idea of success, it's time to work on the roadmap. The roadmap is your plan for getting to the success marker from where you are now. Relationship's a shamble? You might need to detour to a marriage counselor. Work troubles? You might need to think about what you want your career to look like in five years and then consider what will get you there—maybe it's a lateral move within your company or maybe it's getting more education or becoming more assertive. The roadmap doesn't have the exits and stops yet—that's where the goals come in after this. First, focus on the path. Really get to know your path, make sure it is the best path for you. Of course you can always recalculate due to "traffic accidents" or "roadblocks" and "detours," but this is your best guess from where you're standing now. How long do you think the path will take? Are you willing to commit to that time frame? Will this idea of success take you too far away from what you value?

Then go one step further and create the goals themselves. Set reasonable expectations. Give them names and time frames. Make them achievable, and achievable within the time frame you've given yourself. I understand that sometimes we are given unreasonable goals to meet and we must make our best self-discipline efforts to rise to the occasion. But when you do get to set your own goals, set them well. Set yourself up for success. Set goals that inspire you, make forward progress, and keep you on the right track.

Goals should . . .
- Be achievable
- Be given a reasonable time frame
- Move you forward
- Keep you focused

Now we've got good snacks, we're lifting self-discipline weights, and we know what our version of success is, what our values are, how to get there, and what steps to take along the way. Now it's time to make sure we're being our own best keepers.

CHART A ROADMAP

Sketch, chart out, or outline your path to success. Start with a word or picture that represents your idea of success (e.g., "publish my novel"). Then add in the stops along the way (e.g., "join a writing group"), and finally the specific goals (e.g., "complete first five chapters"), along with realistic dates for completing your goals.

CHART A ROADMAP

YOU ARE YOUR OWN SELF: BE YOUR OWN KEEPER

....

You Are Your Own Self

We have to remember that we are our own selves. That means we make our own decisions. We are in charge of the narrative going on inside our own heads, and we are in charge of the actions we take. This is a double-edged sword. It's exciting to be in control of your own destiny, to know you can bring about change in your own life and accomplish great things in the world. But it's tough because we also have to do the dirty work . . . and we don't seem to like telling ourselves no or doing things we don't love. First, let's take a look at all of the positive aspects of being our own selves.

I think the very best part of being one's own self is the power that comes from realizing your internal strength and bravery. This isn't the easiest task, though. You have to take ownership of yourself. We all have some good things and bad things inside us; strengths, weaknesses, positives and negatives. We all have gritty parts of our personalities that like to show when we're stressed or tired. We all have go-to reactions that may not be the best. We all have them, every single one of us, though our lists vary in length and description.

Owning the negative parts of yourself is one of the most useful things you can do for your self-discipline journey. You must really get to know your weaknesses, what makes them tick, when they come out to play, and what makes them quiet down. These are the things that will trip you up in your self-discipline journey time and time again. Know your enemies. Know how to defeat them.

To do this, you'll need to **take stock of your inner self**. It's tough work, it really is. A funny thing about life is we can often divulge things to strangers, but we have a tough time admitting them to ourselves. I'm not sure why; but I know we must work to get through to ourselves. We'll start by visualizing our hearts, a great baseline measurement of our current existence.

Heart Visualization: Quiet yourself. Quiet every part of your being. Turn off your negative inner monologue; relax the muscles behind your eyes; let your limbs feel heavy. Find your center. Then, visualize your heart. Chances are an image will pop into your head immediately; one you might not even understand at first. Capture the image. Look at details, ask it questions, see if it changes. Give it time to fully load and for your mind's eye to fully take it in. Then come back to reality. Use the space below to write down or draw every detail you remember. This is your starting point. What is your heart telling you?

I'll give you some examples: I've seen my heart wrapped in barbed wire, I've seen it buried in concrete, I've seen it

HEART VISUALIZATION

Draw or list all the details you can remember from your heart visualization.

paper-thin, and I've seen it bleeding. I've seen parts closed off, parts broken, parts growing weeds, and parts growing flowers. My subconscious loves this chance to portray unsaid things and to show me its own state of affairs. It's different nearly every time I do this exercise, and it always tells me something deep about my life that was bubbling beneath the surface.

This can be mentally exhausting, as if your mind were pulling dusty files from the back of your brain, so take a walk or drink some tea after you've written or drawn your detailed heart visualization. Then come back to it. What is it speaking to you? Does the barbed wire indicate that you are seeking protection through dangerous means? Do the roots of the weeds go deeply into one area of your life? Did you pour that concrete in or did someone else?

Next, we'll focus on our weaknesses specifically. While the heart visualization probably gave you a good starting point for what to work on in your life, actually naming our weak spots is important. We must give them a name, bring them to the light, let them have their say. Then we can have our say.

To do this, you're going to get a piece of paper and write down every negative thing about yourself that you know is true. You're going to be honest. You're going to write things like, "Critical" and "Judgmental" and "Can't Stand Traffic Jams & Reacts Poorly," but you might use stronger language if that suits you. Everything, big and small.

Then, you're going to ask one trusted friend (not a spouse or family member) to be brutally honest. You're also going to ask them to write down things about yourself that you can work on. I *know* this is hard to do, but we simply *must* have an outsider's perspective. We just have to take this in a spirit of love and self-development. Our friends want to protect us, so they may not have told us these hard things about ourselves. But if you can convince your friend it's in your best interest to hear about what they see in you that needs work, their perspective might change your life—in good ways. Let them know you will handle their responses with the same respect and love with which they offer them.

Cut all of the items into small slips of paper, and add them to a big jar, bucket, or hat. Go to a place where you can safely burn these slips of paper. Read each one out loud. Let it sink in for a moment. Then burn the slip of paper. You have taken away its power. It is gone.

Obviously it isn't gone-gone, but the power it has over your mind is gone. Now every time you want to say something overly judgmental or curse at a slow car or whatever it is for you, you have a mental image of those flames as a reminder that you have power over your negative habits. You can choose whether to indulge them or not.

But it isn't all hard work! Don't lose heart. Now you get to do the fun part of self-discovery—asking far and wide for compliments about your strengths and best qualities. Ask family, friends, coworkers, ask acquaintances and your entire social media list. Ask them to tell you what they think is your best quality. Compile these on notecards, one on each notecard. These are your "notes to self" when you're feeling down. You *are* these things. You are amazing, talented, loved and loving, admired, strong, courageous, and so much more. Take it to heart. Post a few of these on your mirror, your door, and

MY WEAKNESSES

Use this space to list the negative things about yourself that you know are true. Then use the bottom half of the page to list your strengths.

_____

_____

_____

_____

_____

_____

MY STRENGTHS

_____

_____

_____

_____

_____

_____

_____

_____

_____

_____

_____

your refrigerator. Tuck one into your wallet. Tape one on your computer screen.

Is it harder for you to accept your weaknesses or your strengths? I'm not sure why seeing ourselves with a balanced view is incredibly difficult, but it is. We can do it for others, seeing beauty where others might see some rough edges; focusing on good and potential rather than the past and the not-so-great. But we can't take the same measuring stick to ourselves. We blow everything out of proportion, see our flaws big and bold, and brush off our accomplishments. It's time to take ownership of you. All of you. The not-so-great bits that you can work on, and the already-totally-awesome bits that you can rock to their full extent. Self-discipline is here to help.

Be Your Own Keeper

Being your own keeper is something we either learn or don't learn as children, and we can learn it in negative or positive ways.

Some of us have a lot to unlearn when it comes to being our own keeper.

If we were neglected, abandoned, or unloved as children, we probably have a deep-seated sense of self-preservation. Chances are we're proud of this street-smartness we've developed. But it's armor, really. Self-preservation is not self-discipline, much as they mirror each other. Self-preservation is much more primal, much more instinct-based, and it creates a hard shell. We will survive; we must survive, through all means necessary. This can be erosive and destructive as we grow up and our need for self-preservation lessens in actuality, but not in our veins and brains. We are coded somehow to always look out for number one, to always put our needs first, to do whatever it takes to get something we need or want. You can see how this leads to burnout at best, and illegal actions at worst. It is no way to live life. So we'll try to calm those primordial urges and let them know they will be taken care of—but perhaps not first, perhaps not now. That is self-discipline.

If we were criticized deeply or pushed hard to prove ourselves and succeed as children, self-discipline is probably something familiar to us. But this is a twisted version of self-discipline, one I like to call self-approval. It's this incurable need for approval, from ourselves and others. Perfection is the goal, always, end of story. If perfection can't be achieved, we usually abandon the task out of fear of failure. While we think this is a self-protective measure, it's actually holding us back. We cannot soar to new heights unless we push through failure, cannot discover new lands unless we try things we've never done before. Our comfort zone of perfection is actually a cage of criticism. So we'll calm that voice that says we aren't good enough and instead we'll listen to the louder one that says, "Grow!" That is self-discipline.

We can also be nurtured too much, and lulled into a sense of self-accomplishment. Everything we do is amazing, everything we do is wonderful. On one hand, self-discipline comes easily because we think everything we do turns out fabulously, so we keep doing it. On the other hand, this is disillusionment and can eventually hurt our souls deeply when we find out the truth: We are not perfect, and not everything we do is amazing. This is *life*, and it is true for *everyone*. We are flawed hearts beating in fleshly bodies, and we fail. And that is okay. But if we have never been taught how to fail well, self-accomplishment will be our downfall. So let's look honestly at results, let's take criticism well, let's learn to grow through all circumstances, let's know when to push ourselves to pursue better. That is self-discipline.

I think there are very few individuals who grow up with a healthy level of self-discipline. Those who do have a leg up on everything in life, because they've learned the delicate balance of self and discipline that makes their world go 'round. They know the peaks and valleys, the shortcuts and the long ways round and when to take each, and they know their reserve of nourishment and fuel so they can pace themselves. They are not afraid to be beginners, but they come prepared. They are humble but sure, exacting but flexible, curious but focused. This doesn't come easily. It's a process of trial and error. We have to find our own self-discipline equilibrium, and that's what this book will help you do.

We've grown up, we're adults now, and no matter how our perception of self-discipline has found its way into our psyche, there is good news. We can change it. We can mold it. We can learn to be good keepers of our time and energy. Being your own keeper is basically kindergarten all over again, except that you are the student *and* the teacher. You have to be the one to set snack time, know when you need a nap, and most important, know when you need a time out. In this case, I actually mean that we need snack times, nap or rest times, and time outs, even as adults. We get so busy and focused on deadlines that we forget to eat or can't shut off our brains to sleep . . . this is no way to accomplish our best work. Tired, *hangry* adults only turn in subpar results. And they still tend to throw tantrums, though they are likely to be less kicking-on-the-floor and more taking-it-out-on-everyone-else.

The Basics: Basics come first in my self-discipline map. Eating well, making time for exercise, sleeping well, and making time for family and friends. These are the nonnegotiables of self-discipline. They take self-discipline to accomplish, yes, but they are the building blocks for it, as well. Building anything requires different kinds of blocks, different structures for different angles, and different materials for different applications. So we need a toolbox, a map, a warehouse of building materials. Self-discipline is not its own thing with its own capabilities. It is something we create, because we are our own keepers. And being your own keeper is like digging the basement and setting it in concrete. The rest goes on top, and without it, you're sunk. Take responsibility for your actions, pick up the toolbelt, and let's take a look at some of the tools in the map . . . errr . . . tools in the toolbox, markers on the map, blocks in the warehouse.

Taking Responsibility: Responsibility. No one really loves the word, or the meaning. It brings with it implications of drudgery, picking up the negative tasks that no one wants to do, and taking them on. Well, yes. Some of this happens. It's part of life and we have to be team players, and every once in a while, we each get the drudgery. But we are also responsible for ourselves and our actions. That means we must do the drudgery in our own lives; must do the hard things that take more work. Trust me, I love taking life easy, seeing what comes, and lounging as I wait for it. This is fun for a while, but in the end, it merely seeps into my bones and I become lazy. I forget what is important to me. I forget what I want to do, what I came here to accomplish. I forget that I want to be healthy, happy, fulfilled in life, instead of *waiting* to see what *might* come. Take responsibility for your life. Take up the cause of change. You are worth it.

Taking responsibility means knowing what's good for you and what isn't. It's not fun, but it's part of self-discipline. I love donuts, loooovvve them, but I know they aren't good for me for breakfast. For dessert, yes. But when I start my day with a donut, it's all downhill from there—blood sugar tanks about an hour after the sugar high wears off, and it isn't pretty until I get a full meal to balance the sugar craziness. That's only part of it. I know donuts are bad for me. I could switch to slightly-less-sugary muffins. But I also know that my body loves vegetables and protein in the morning. Avocado is its favorite thing. It takes time to cook an egg and slice an avocado and throw some salsa on it. But the few minutes I spend in the morning frying up an egg is worth it because my entire day is more balanced and I am more focused. For me, part of being self-disciplined means every morning eating protein and vegetables, because my body does its best work with that fuel.

Grace and Gratitude

It's all well and good to be our own keepers, but we have to remember there is this thing in life called grace. Oh my, what a nice cool breeze it is in our lives. Grace doesn't always come from the external sources we wish it did. Goodness, we wish our bosses gave grace when we were a few minutes late, we wish our spouses gave a bit more grace when we messed up. But we can't control grace from others in our lives. We can, however, control the grace we allow ourselves in our own lives. Give yourself grace when you fail a little, when you accidentally take two steps back, when someone doesn't like the way you're doing your life. You are a work in progress; that's why you're reading this book. You're here on this earth to learn, and remember, none of us are leaving having perfected it, so give yourself a little extra margin. You are the only you you get, so be kind.

Gratitude is another cool breeze on the road of self-discipline. Be thankful for the things you have. Focus on the here and now, the things you can hold in your hands and the things you can hold in your heart. Let these blessings fill you up inside and let you know you are strong, you are loved, you are wanted. You are here. If you ever feel in need of a boost, make a gratitude list. List everything that you are grateful for, big and small . . . health, sunrises, coffee, family, a job, pink pens, friends, and did I mention coffee?

MY GRATITUDE LIST

CURIOSITY IS THE NEW VULNERABILITY

....

Curiosity is your superpower. Most people seeking self-discipline completely disregard the role that curiosity plays. Curiosity helps you create your own brand of success, helps you be flexible when faced with self-discipline hurdles, helps you create your own self-discipline masterpiece.

Vulnerability has had its shining moment in the spotlight as a secret sauce for success and breaking out of your own shell and comfort zone. Yes, vulnerability is valuable. But I declare that curiosity is here as the new buzzword of self-discipline. Curiosity fuels self-discipline in all of the ways vulnerability can but goes even deeper.

Vulnerability is self-oriented, whereas curiosity is externally focused. We need this external focus even though self-discipline is internal at its base. Internal-only focus will get us only so far, and believe me, it's not very far. An internal focus is selfish and narrow-minded, only after what we can "use" rather than what we can do, what we can learn, what can help us grow, what we can give to others.

When we focus externally, when we are excited to sniff out the next big thing, to find the next grand idea, we have purpose.

Curiosity is the quickest way to create purpose. Curiosity is open. Open mind, open heart, open eyes. Curiosity is not selfish, it doesn't "use" others, doesn't expect things to be given to it. Curiosity gives work meaning, which in turn gives self-discipline some grip. Curiosity creates forward motion. Curiosity gives us something to strive for; it gives us an endgame.

Curiosity is what makes us say, "Well, what if we put in a skylight up here?" or "What if I took my show on the road?" *What if* is such an enticing phrase, such an open-ended beginning. Curiosity opens career paths, cures cancer, inspires artists, and makes the world a drastically better place. It is also, in its own way, a form of vulnerability. Curiosity means accepting that you don't have all the answers, all the tools, all the ideas. It means being willing to do something differently, which takes deep strength and self-assurance and a willingness to fail. Curiosity enables us to fail better. "I have not failed," said the ever-curious Thomas Edison. "I've just found 10,000 ways that won't work."

Curiosity is what makes us strive to be better human beings, to learn more, grow, share, and seek out value and value-adding activities for our lives. What better way is there to ensure we *want* to do the things we do? There's a difference, you know, between wanting to do something in theory and wanting to do it in reality. Curiosity is the tightrope between the two, and we have to walk it to make anything happen. Curiosity doesn't make things happen in and of itself. Self-discipline does that. But self-discipline only focuses on the self and the discipline if it doesn't have curiosity to open its eyes and show it the world.

We have to diligently seek evocative situations in our lives that cultivate creativity. We can all be curious, and we can all develop the habit of intentional curiosity. There are plenty of ways to go about it, and none of them are wrong.

Change Your Environment: Physically leaving our usual space is a good way to start. Work from a coworking space instead of your cubicle. Spend the night in a hotel, even if it's five miles down the road. Changing your environment, simple as it is, changes what you see. Whom you see. How you see it. Wake up somewhere new, get coffee somewhere new, heck, "cross the pond" on Queen Mary II or take a train across the country if you can. Traveling outside of your normal route is a sure-fire way to create curiosity, because it puts you smack-dab in the middle of it. This helps you to become curious about how others do the same things you do. *(The Brits have a totally different way of looking at the world. I adore it. Cross the pond for a week or two, or spend a weekend at a bed-and-breakfast. I think bed-and-breakfasts are about as close to being in England as we have here in America.)*

Look Backwards: Notice I said *look* backwards, not *move* backwards. Looking at the past can often inform our future in a meaningful way. Context is what we find when we're curious about the past. We might find context for our new marketing campaigns, context about what it was like to raise a family a few generations back in our family tree, or context about what really set us on fire when we were kids, before the world told us what we should be. This is valuable information. This helps you become curious about your past and your present. *(Interview your grandparents or parents if you're lucky enough to have them still alive. Really listen to what they say. How can you apply it to your life?)*

Expand Your Scope: Expanding your scope means enlarging your circle of influence and experience. Volunteering is a great value-adding activity that incites curiosity in your world. Even better, it adds value to others' lives, too. Join a board (I know, I know, more meetings, but if you offer value, you receive value). Join a cause. Run for local government. Champion foster parents, pet adoption, cancer research. Walk for juvenile diabetes or March of Dimes or Big Brothers Big Sisters. Find something that excites you and get involved. This helps you become curious about people and their stories. *(I guarantee your life will improve if you expand your scope by volunteering. Stop by the local humane society this weekend. Bring dog food and a few dog treats to donate. Don't do this out of duty, but with a spirit of helpfulness and investment. See the change you can make with $20 and 20 minutes.)*

Plant Seeds: This is similar to networking, but networking looks to gain something, whereas planting seeds is an exercise in curiosity. Planting seeds means creating connections and being genuinely open to seeing what sprouts up. A lot of times when you plant seeds, you aren't the one to see the results. Someone else gets to reap the reward, but they wouldn't be able to unless someone (you!) planted a seed. Genuinely, freely, without expectation . . . like a child, curious to see things root and grow. Think about the future. Focus on planting seeds

CURIOSITY SPARKS

Use this space to reflect on your past or to list places you want to explore, people to meet with, or classes to try.

_____

_____

_____

_____

_____

_____

_____

_____

_____

_____

_____

_____

_____

_____

_____

_____

_____

_____

_____

_____

_____

and be curious about the future. Bonus: You get to harvest the seeds that others have planted, too. Circle of life, baby. *(Literally plant some seeds. Engage in the process. Get your hands in some dirt, get a little messy, and then see the reward. When we have a physical visual, we can do the metaphorical version better in real life. Once you see leaves, go plant some seeds in your life so they can grow together, reminding you of how beautiful life is.)*

Climb Higher: Everyone can see the low-hanging fruit, and they're all fighting over it. No need to join the competition, because you're a creative and curious person, aren't you? Climb higher, grab a ladder, get an apple picker, strap on a berry basket. See if there's anything ripe on the tall branches. What can you see from up there? See how the sun sets over the gentle hills and see that there are orchards in the distance, too, perhaps with more delicious fruit. A change in perspective is often enough to send curiosity skyrocketing, even if you've been picking fruit from this orchard your whole life. There is always more to be found (see "The Falsity of Scarcity," page 175). This helps you become curious about possibility. *(Meet with someone who is a few stages of life or work ahead of you, and ask if they'd be your mentor. This is a great way to see the higher view, to see the "could be" and the "someday" in the distance, and to have a helping hand to get there.)*

Try Something New: Take a yoga class instead of TRX. Listen to a different radio station, take a different route to work, try a new lunch place. Go to the opera, or a megaplex 3-D movie theater, whichever is different from your normal. Normal is the death of curiosity. Be disciplined in trying new things, because new things spark new ideas. Things get flowing in a new way, new neurons get firing in our brains, and we are suddenly filled with energy. *(Try a new coffee shop and bring along a notebook. Something about a hot beverage, people watching, and empty pages inspire creativity. Write a journal entry, a poem, a to-do list, a list of dreams for the future . . . let creativity flow.)*

How to Avoid Lone-Wolf Syndrome: The Lone-Wolf Syndrome is a popular, often self-inflicted illness found in the seekers of self-discipline. They forget everything and everyone that isn't on their immediate mind. They have laser vision on their goals, on what they simply *must* accomplish. They must and they will. These are your at-all-costs people, the lone wolves who avoid the pack because the pack will supposedly hold them back. They think the pack is competition, or sometimes, they don't even realize there's a pack they could join. They are too hungry to think of anyone but themselves. This may result in some impressive conquests early on. Lone wolves have only one tool in their toolkit, and it's not enough when the going gets tough. Lone wolves forget to be curious about life's possibilities because they are so self-focused. They aren't vulnerable enough to do life in community. That, in the end, is their weakness and their downfall.

We are pack animals, both wolves and humans. We crave companionship and are designed to do life together. There is a proverb that says, "If you want to go fast, go alone. If you want to go far, go together." Growing, sharing, seeking out value, adding value . . . these are not things that can be accomplished alone. Being curious about life involves other people.

What's the cure, you might ask? Well, of course, the things listed above on how to be curious will help because they push you out of your comfort zone and into the circle of community. Really, the only medicine here is social medicine. Be curious about life outside of yourself and your own goals. Find a class, a conference, a church, or a community event to go to. Be present, be all in, and chances are, you'll find others who are there for the same reasons. These are probably your pack people. Build your pack. Look close (friends, family) and look far (mentors, inspirational figures). Purposefully connect. Ask them out for coffee. Exchange emails and social media contacts. It can be awkward at first, but then you'll get the hang of it. Engage with them out of curiosity: What is their life like right now? What are they struggling with? What can you help them with? What is exciting them right now? Be interested in the answers and see if you can offer any value to them.

Lone wolves don't generally like to offer things. They keep the food they find for themselves and aren't keen on sharing. But creative curiosity demands sharing and offering. Be part of the cycle. Offer and create and be a person others want to get to know. Cultivate a depth of self. Be you, but know that other people can accept you. You needn't keep your head down on this path to self-discipline alone. You can walk with others. You can, I promise. Try it.

Making Time for Curiosity: I know you're going to say you don't have time for all of this curiosity stuff. You have *things* to *accomplish*, that's why you're here. But I don't believe the things you accomplish will stick or take you very far if you don't have creativity to back them up. Schedule time for creativity. Put it on your calender: "Get out of the office for 30 mins or an hour." Or "Go to the orchard this weekend with the family." You can also join groups in your community through websites like MeetUp, VolunteerMatch, RSVP, and SCORE. Seek and you will find. The resources are limitless; you just have to take the time to find the connection that works for you.

Curiosity is the giver of so much of our vital energy. It is imperative we keep the curiosity tank full, because when it goes empty, we are liable to lose our momentum. And momentum is imperative.

MILK YOUR MOMENTUM: MAINTAIN AND MUSCLE THROUGH

··················

Ahh, energy, that beloved self-discipline friend-foe. We love it when we have, and we hate it when we don't. How do we get more of it? We milk our momentum, baby.

Energy is a hallmark of self-discipline. Self-discipline runs on it, craves it, and seems to drain it rather fast. Then again, self-discipline becomes its own form of energy when traditional motivation runs dry. Learning to create a closed-loop system of energy is key for cultivating self-discipline. What does that mean? A closed-loop energy system means that energy leaks are eliminated and extra energy is funneled back into the system. Nothing is lost. What does that look like in real life? Here's how to milk momentum, maintain perspective, and muscle through when things get hard.

Milk Momentum

Momentum is a wonderful thing. Momentum, in my vocabulary, is hard work paying off and paying forward. Momentum is, again, that best of all self-discipline friends, motion. What starts momentum? Anything going forward. This is the beginning of the energy system, and we have to light the fire somehow. Even the tiniest step begets momentum, and it turns into a baby step, then two baby steps, and eventually leaps and bounds. Even if the steps don't grow, and they remain tiny baby steps, they are still building upon one another, still taking you forward. Luckily, they tend to snowball, in a good way. Milking momentum means taking these little steps and making each one work toward your goal as effectively as it possibly can.

Get off the Hamster Wheel: One of your main tasks is to prevent hamster-wheel syndrome. There are two strains of hamster-wheel syndrome. One is making all sorts of racket and using up all of your energy by going in circles. This looks like fun. It looks like progress. But it is doing nothing but wearing you out. The second strain is the "hold on for dear life" maneuver that happens when you get going too fast on the hamster wheel. The momentum is *more* than you can handle, so you have no choice but to hold on for dear life and let the hamster wheel spin *you* around by force until it comes to a slow halt, throwing you off on the side, dizzy and disoriented. The only cure for either of these is to stay off the hamster wheel. This is why you must have a plan.

Have a Plan: Knowing what step is next takes the pressure off and prevents both hamster-wheel syndromes. It's basically a B-12 shot to momentum. A plan allows you to focus on the next task without thinking about it. This can be simple things, such as your morning routine or meal planning, or it can be big things, such as marketing plan implementation and an editorial calendar. Things get done when they're planned. If you can automate these things, even better. Anything we can automate on the road to self-discipline is a win.

Automate as Much As You Can: Automation oils the gears of momentum. It makes everything easier. Automation delegates without the agony of constant decision making. Automation oils the gears because once things are turning, if you automate them, they keep turning without you there to crank the wheel. What can you automate? Things like auto-pay bills, auto-reorder supplies . . . auto-anything that they offer you, sign up for it, if it is something that would normally take your time or effort. This is free time in your time bank. Other life-things can be automated by you, such as knowing you only grocery shop during the 7–8 a.m. hour on Wednesday mornings because that is the slowest time at the grocery store, allowing you to maximize your time. You won't be tempted to get on the hamster wheel of shopping when you feel like it or need something. Chances are you will feel like it or need something more than once a week, which is a time drain if you haven't planned.

Maintain Perspective

Maintaining perspective is one of the hardest parts of milking momentum, because no matter how exciting it is to see results, our energy cannot be at a constant high. Instead of running a sprint, we have to run a marathon here. Maintaining in this case means making sure our basics are taken care of, that we have systems in place to prevent burnout, and that we are able to delegate and use our energy for our most effective tasks.

Be Aware of Your Basics: It's funny that we apply "self-discipline" to the big things, the earth-shaking things, but often forget to apply it to the basics, like eating well, going to the gym, sleeping enough, and spending time with our family and friends—all things mentioned before. These help us keep molehills as molehills, help us function at our best, and help us keep our one and only self-discipline instrument—ourselves—in tip-top shape. Don't forget—your brain likes snacks. Feed your brain snacks. Have you noticed I'm a big proponent of snacks?

Build in Margin: Things take longer than usual. It's just a fact of life. It is very rare that we find ourselves saying, "Well, that didn't take nearly as long as I expected!" or "That wasn't nearly as expensive as I expected!" The opposite is usually true. Build in margins of error. Pad time and cost estimates to manage expectations, both your expectations and those of others.

Systems to Prevent Burnout: How do we prevent burnout? By creating systems to prevent it. This is difficult when there's a world to conquer, I know. The world doesn't sleep, but we need sleep to be able to conquer it. Schedule breaks. Schedule yoga, massages, time with friends, schedule down-time and dream-time. Schedule brain-dumping sessions and brainstorming sessions, to get rid of the old and create the new.

Delegating: Delegating tasks or outsourcing them is an effective tool for creating balance in business and life. We all need to delegate or outsource tasks. No one, no matter how self-disciplined, can do all the things all of the time. We must focus our vital energy (the very best we have to offer) on the things that require it. Hiring others to do tasks that are not an effective use of our vital energy is critical for preserving momentum and not getting mired in details. Trust others, and move forward.

What is Vital Energy? *Vital energy is your metaphorical life force; the very best your soul and spirit have to offer. It's the extra life you have to spill into the world, so it must be used with care. Spill wisely, my friends. Vital energy can be overwhelming if spilled out too quickly, and is hardly vital when it is dripped reluctantly on projects. Vital energy is life-giving and must be poured into life-giving things. Sometimes our vital energy levels get low, and sometimes they're running high. Protecting vital energy levels is a task that must be done with vigilance.*

Practice Perspective: All of the above items will help you maintain perspective. But you can also practice keeping perspective by looking at progress numbers, reading biographies of successful people in your field, and simply by being open to the natural course that life takes us on no matter how well delegated and planned-out we are. We have to keep the perspective that we are not in control of all things. We cannot manipulate the universe. Life happens. That is a magical, wonderful thing we must embrace if we plan to master this self-discipline thing.

Muscle Through

Sometimes the only way to make self-discipline work is to muscle through. That means taking all of your deep-down reserves and pushing forward when your mind is tired, your body is exhausted, and there seem to be roadblocks all around you. Muscling through is what sets the self-discipline amateurs and professionals apart. Amateurs give up when momentum slows and energy wanes. Professionals? Professionals know that there is always—always—more to be found. Where is it, though? How come only some people know the secret code to access this "more"?

There is no secret code. Only you know what surges through your veins and goes to the place of "more"—it's different for each of us and that's a good thing. If we could go to the gym and work our "muscle through" muscles, everyone would be doing it. But the only way to work these muscles is to do it, and the more you muscle through, the stronger you become. Realizing this secret depth exists within you is incredibly transformative.

Is muscling through the same thing as beating your head against a brick wall? No. That's the definition of insanity—"doing the same thing over and over again expecting different results." And self-discipline is not insanity. In fact, it is an imaginative kind of sane, if that can be a thing, in that it is always seeking new alternatives and new ways of doing things to achieve different results. Self-discipline doesn't see no. Self-discipline sees maybe and not yet. Self-discipline sees, "Let me see what I can do."

Muscling through is figuring out how to chip away at the brick, how to jackhammer through it, jump over it, skydive to the other side, or stage a protest to have the wall taken down. Perspective is important in figuring out the best way to muscle through. Truth is, sometimes the best way to muscle through is to acknowledge the wall, tell it, "I see you, and I am not forgetting you," but to focus on another aspect of the project. Things have a way of moving themselves when we keep moving.

What to Do When You're Leaking Energy: As hard as we try to create a closed-loop system, we'll probably find an energy drain here and there. When you find you can't maintain momentum and muscling through isn't working, energy begins to drain. When this happens, it can be easy to want to shut down the whole system, systematically find it, fix it, and restart. This takes a lot of effort and is a last-ditch idea rather than a go-to solution. Stopping the system, or giving up/quitting, is a death knell to self-discipline. When we're leaking energy we need to seek help, and we need to seek help fast. Have no fear, advice and help are scary words, but they are friends of self-discipline.

HUMILITY IS HARD: HELP IS REQUIRED

....

Humility. It's a word we don't like much these days, especially when it comes to *self*-discipline. But humility and
self-discipline are not opposites. They cannot be opposites if
we want to be successful human beings. I want to be a successful human being, no matter what it takes. Don't you?

Humility and self-discipline need each other to thrive. It is
a symbiotic relationship. If humility is left on its own, it can
become a door-mat of everyone else's priorities, feelings, and
accomplishments. If self-discipline is left on its own, it stomps
its boots hard on that doormat. When the two work together,
great things are accomplished. Humility with self-discipline
creates a potent combination that allows us to keep a broader focus and to accomplish things with the help of a team. It
helps us recognize that self-discipline is not an "at all costs"
thing. There are costs to self-discipline, and some are too steep
to pay. Humility helps us recognize these.

Make no mistake, humility is hard. Just look around . . .
you'll find that few have decided to undertake the challenge of
humility. It means admitting that somehow, someway, we aren't
all that we think we are. It means that maybe, actually, the world

doesn't revolve around us. Well, truth is, none of us are everything. None of us are perfect. Perfection does not exist in this world, so we can stop striving for it. It is a useless game. Once we let go of perfection (remember, this isn't self-perfection, only self-discipline we're talking about), we can embrace humility.

Why does humility help us? Doesn't humility make us weak?

No. Humility makes us human. Does being human make us weak? No. It is our strength. Humility means that we can act with empathy, that we can make decisions with our hearts, that we can value humanity, love and accept it, and embrace it wholeheartedly. But that's not our first inclination sometimes. We prefer to go it alone. To use our heads. To tell risk to take a hike and to protect our hearts at all costs from danger and disappointment. We don't like different, we don't like accepting we are wrong sometimes, and we do not like admitting that maybe, just maybe, we could use a little help.

When we know that humility doesn't make us weak, it follows that asking for help doesn't make us weak. If we need another set of hands to accomplish a task, does that mean the task isn't worth accomplishing? Absolutely not. Humility is hard, but help is required.

Getting Help

Help, in the form of a counselor, therapist, or deeply patient friend, may be required to get to a point of humility. Taking care of your mental and emotional fortitude is a form of strength, as well. We are not all given the gift of deep humility and empathy as our natural manner of being. Most of us have to learn how to accomplish these things. Seeing a therapist forces you to get really-really honest about yourself. There's pretty much no way to hide from them; they see right through all of your walls and will ask the most carefully crafted questions that get at the deeper issues and expose us. That's their job. It's like a surgeon who has to cut open the healthy flesh to get to the diseased flesh . . . we all have unhealthy parts in our psyche, and therapists are the doctors. There is no shame in this. We are blessed to live in a time when the stigma of mental illness is being heartily chipped away at, rightfully so. Brains get sick, too. Hearts get hurt, too. They need bandages and doctors and even medicine.

Of course, getting help is not a quick fix. I know those of us who thrive on self-discipline are quick-fix junkies. We want it done right and done now. But humility is a deep heart-thing, and there are no shortcuts when it comes to those. Finding humility will probably mean accepting limitations you don't even want to admit you face. It might mean giving up things you thought were priorities. You might be broken in areas you thought were your strongest. It will likely require a lot of forgiveness, both giving and accepting. It might mean revisiting some difficult places in your past to deal with them. Getting to a place of humility will likely be a gut punch of reality, and those are not fun. But persevere, for it is only the strong who get up after a gut punch, who keep fighting and win.

How to Practice Humility

Like just about everything in the self-discipline toolkit, humility is something we need to practice. Of course we can wait until we are handed a situation that takes us down a few pegs and makes us face humility whether we like it or not. But that is actually the hard way, even though it might seem like the easy way. Letting ourselves go until we must face the music is cowardly, the opposite of humility and self-discipline. So we face the prospect of humility head-on, cultivate it, and seek to live our lives in a humble state. Remember, humility is strength.

As I said earlier, most of us are not born with a humble spirit. Most of our first words involve, "No!" "Me!" and "Mine!" Sharing does not come easily. Sacrifice is not in our vocabularies. We are the stars of the show, and that show must go on. This might work when we're two, but then we must add "Yours," "Ours," and "Yes" and try to say those words more than we say the first three.

Sharing is one of the most important parts of life to master as we get older. Sacrifice is an even deeper heart-thing that doesn't come easily. We are not the stars of the show. So we smile and offer the last cookie, the better work project, the bigger piece of the pie, the recognition we deserve, the time we had set aside for something else. We discipline ourselves to share, to give, to offer. And when we do this more frequently, we see the cycle that happens: what we give comes back to us in more abundance. We give recognition wholeheartedly, only to find it heaped back upon us. We give the last cookie and find a whole box of cookies or a home-baked pie at our doorstep.

A note of caution: We must not do this on the premise that we will get something better. We must do it for the giving aspect, and with a heart open to receiving, but not one that expects. Expectation is never humble.

PRACTICING HUMILITY

List ways you can practice humility in your own life and areas that could use improvement. Be specific, use names and list actions you can complete now or in the near future.

_____

_____

_____

_____

_____

_____

_____

_____

_____

_____

_____

_____

_____

_____

_____

_____

_____

_____

_____

_____

_____

_____

Practicing humility is just like any other practice: sometimes we nail it, and sometimes we fail it. Humility that nails it is honest, true, and not focused on any particular outcome. Humility that fails the practice test is false, leaning into bragging or self-deprecation, and is focused on achieving a particular outcome. Each day, find one way to practice humility. This may mean accepting help from a colleague on a tough work project when you view them as competition. It may mean picking up groceries on your way home from work for your spouse even when you're bone-tired. It may mean giving some verbal praise for something they did, when you'd rather take the credit yourself. Practice, and practice some more. See what happens when you do.

Humility as Self-Love

Humility is actually an act of self-love, too. When we free ourselves from perfection, when we live life in a state of humility, we can accept and give so much more love. Humility is best for our hearts and minds, because it allows us to handle failure and rejection. Softer hearts are stronger hearts. Softer hearts make wholehearted decisions. They follow their gut instincts. Softer hearts are secure enough to take risks in stride, to put themselves out there, to realize that when all is apparently lost, they are not.

The people in our lives won't necessarily benefit from the majority of our self-discipline efforts. Humility, though, benefits the people around us. Humility is a rich soil for love to grow in. Soft hearts are always recognized, always appreciated. Your parents, spouse, roommates, children, and coworkers will all see a change. It may scare them at first. Humility on the heels of pride can be tough to sort out. But when they realize it's real, all will be well.

Now keep in mind that humility does not mean self-abasement. Humility does not mean rejecting pride outright. Humility takes the edge off pride, puts pride in its rightful place. Self-abasement is never healthy, so be careful that in your self-discipline regimen you take care to keep humility on the healthy side of the spectrum. Pride in a job well done is admirable. Pride in seeing a long-haul project to completion, pride at being recognized for your hard-earned work is good. Pride of self, pride that takes over our hearts and makes our decisions for us, is not good. This sort of pride is fear in camouflage.

Soft hearts handle situations from a grounded perspective, instead of from fear.

Fear and Self-Discipline

It's pretty hard for fear and humility to coexist, because humility is all about grace. Fear and grace are enemies. Grace is a self-discipline friend, and fear is a foe. Fear consumes self-discipline and spits it back out, gnarled and worse for the wear. It's funny because we think self-discipline runs on fear. The unhealthy kind of self-discipline does, the kind that grinds us to a pulp and leaves us a shell of our former selves, with no life in our eyes at all. That is not the art of self-discipline. That is self-flagellation through fear.

Self-discipline that runs on humility is unstoppable, because there is literally nothing holding it back, not even fear of failure.

Fear of failure may drive us to be successful for a while, but at the end of the day, success doesn't keep you warm at night. And you have to live with yourself, knowing that the only reason you accomplished your task is because you were scared of the "what if" of failure. Take away the negative "what if" and replace it with its positive form. *What if?* What if we accomplished more than we ever dreamed of? What if we can take this all the way and still feel good in our souls, still have our families by our side, still sleep at night and still look ourselves in the face in the mirror in the morning? That's the sort of *what if* humility creates. A sense of excitement through security and self-love.

Getting rid of fear can be tough. Internal fears are often deep-seated and long-held. We learn fear when we are young, when we are told no, when we are rejected. So fear and humility are deeply connected foes. Writing your fears down and letting them go into the ocean, or burning them to ashes, can be a physical reminder of the mental leap of faith you've taken. Live without fear. You can do it.

The Yes and No of Humility

Believe it or not, how we utilize our "yes" and "no" in our lives is also a sign of our humility, or a symptom of the lack of it. Most of us have a hard time using our yes and no with equilibrium. We are either YES people or NO people. Some of us could do with a few "maybes" of possibility. A few soft yeses when we're scared and a few hard nos when they're needed.

Humility allows us to use our yes and no honestly. We can say no without fear of letting others down. Likewise, we can say yes with full intention and commitment.

YES AND NO WORKSHEET

Take stock of the things in your life right now. What could use a little more yes from your heart? What could use a little stricter no from your mind?

_____

_____

_____

_____

_____

_____

_____

_____

_____

_____

_____

_____

_____

_____

_____

_____

_____

_____

_____

_____

_____

HONE YOUR HUSTLE: DON'T DABBLE

....

When it comes to self-discipline, we think we must do it all, do it all now, and do it all well. That is a recipe for certain burn-out. Now that we know we can tackle our self-discipline practice with humility, and without fear, we realize we can specialize. We can hone our hustle. We don't need to do it all, now, well. We can do us, masterfully, with constant improvement. That's the art of self-discipline. Honing your hustle means letting go of the extraneous things that we do "just because." We might do them "just because" they make us money, they give us prestige, they make us feel good about ourselves, they impress someone else, etc. The list of "just because" reasons is long and complicated. It's also just a list of excuses. Yes, I just called you out on it, and I can, because my list of excuses was once just as long.

A lot of us who come to study the art of self-discipline are good at a lot of things. Things just come easily to us, so we don't necessarily feel the need to be self-disciplined, to plan ahead, to get things done ahead of time and perfected. When last-minute gets us A+s and Employee of the Week, why should we muster up any more of our precious creative energy?

MY JUST BECAUSE LIST

List the things that you say yes to or do "just because" and the ways you think you could challenge yourself to either find purpose in them or really hone them down to what matters most.

_____

_____

_____

_____

_____

_____

_____

_____

_____

_____

_____

_____

_____

_____

_____

_____

_____

_____

_____

_____

_____

_____

_____

Well, the truth is, or at least *my* truth is, that I don't use that creative energy for all of the projects I say I will. I dwindle that creative energy by shopping, watching television, fiddling on my phone, and doing just about anything other than actually channeling it productively. In other words, it goes to waste. All of the beautiful creative energy of mine, that I could be using to change the world, gets mired in the mud and quicksand of laziness.

I *want* to be self-disciplined, but my artist self has been conditioned to think that the muse comes at the last minute and the muse always does good enough to get by.

Get by. Oh, that is the laziness talking. And I get lazy when I've spread myself too thin. When my project list is a mile long, my list of excuses becomes two miles long. Of course, laziness is the opposite of self-discipline. Self-discipline never says how do I "get by," because self-discipline is reaching for "get beyond the stars."

So how do we bridge the gap?

Don't dabble. What is dabbling? Dabbling is doing a little of this, a little of that, half-heartedly exploring one option while letting our energy for other things become thinner and thinner. Dabbling is something we all love to do, because we learn to say "yes" and we have curious minds and we are people for whom most everything comes easily to us, so why not try it? Why not add another meeting or product line or van pool to our schedule?

Why not? Because our time and our creative capital are precious commodities. We cannot get these back. What we spend them on is either an investment in our future or a waste of time. Look at the big picture. Look at the details. What is working for you, and what isn't?

What is Creative Capital? *Our "creative capital" as I call it is our very own precious blend of life experiences, dreams, imaginings, and the way we do our day-to-day life. It is the backbone of any creative endeavor, it's what makes the poetry poetic, the lyrics lyrical, the story believable. Even if your pursuit is not creative in nature, creative capital keeps you inventive. Creative capital is what gives you an edge in any (yes, any) field.*

How to Hone Your Hustle

I love the word hone. It has such a comforting long "o" to it that makes it sound simple and old-fashioned. Honing means to sharpen or smooth. While it is an old-fashioned concept (the idea of honing with a whetstone), the idea is not so simple. Honing something nowadays means tuning it, going right to the heart of the matter and putting every last little piece in place just-so. To sharpen up the corners, or to smooth them out—knowing which one to do is where the real genius lies. Here's how to hone your hustle.

Make a Goal: What is your main hustle goal? A hustle is what you put your energy, your heart, and your passion into, be it work, a side-gig you're trying to get off the ground, your family, or your research. Your hustle is your heart-work. It's usually hard work, as well, and requires all your self-discipline tricks. Now is the time to up-level. What's the next level for you?

Make a List: Make a physical list on paper. This way you have to force your brain to process as it comes through your hand to the ink. Then you have to force your brain to read it again. To read it aloud. To read it to an accountability partner. The things that are working, that's your hustle. The things that aren't? Dabbling. Strike through the dabbling tasks and commitments and projects. What are you left with? Do these items seem similar? Do they help you achieve your goals? Do they give back in a measure equal to or better than what you put into them?

HUSTLES AND DABBLES

List the interests that take up your time. Cross off the things that you do halfheartedly, the things you aren't really passionate about. Then cross off the things that just don't seem to be working for you. What's left? It's probably your hustle, and it probably deserves your focus far more than all the other things on your list.

_____

_____

_____

_____

_____

_____

_____

_____

_____

_____

_____

_____

_____

_____

_____

_____

_____

_____

What is an Accountability Partner? *An accountability partner is someone who has agreed to help you on your journey. Chances are, you're helping them on theirs, but maybe not. Choose someone whose opinion you trust, and whose voice you can listen to, even when they tell you hard things. Approach them with your goal, and ask that they keep you accountable to achieving it. This might mean you set a schedule for check-ins and mini-goals and coffee dates. Or it might mean that they shoot you a text periodically and ask how things are going, and you have to tell them the really-true truth about how things are going.*

Make a Plan: Now that you can see clearly where you should be spending your time and vital energy, you can begin to make a plan. The plan focuses on the specific steps, and the dates by which you will accomplish the steps, to make your goal a reality. The complexity of the plan will depend on the complexity of the goal. Make sure each step is manageable. Give it a deadline that feels comfortable, but not too comfortable. You want to push yourself to be actively productive. Too long of a deadline will increase the likelihood of procrastination. Too close of a deadline will increase the likelihood of a breakdown, which I don't recommend. Choose a realistic time frame that you can complete with competence and confidence.

Make Some "Blinders": Blinders are an important part of our self-discipline routine because the world is constantly sending other things into our field of vision. Companies pay millions of dollars to compete for our mind-space in every possible arena. Children seem to innately master a barrage of distraction tactics to keep us from focusing on anything. Coworkers only seem to have time-sensitive questions just as we settle in to tackle a difficult task. You need blinders. Physical and mental blinders are both helpful. Physical blinders include headphones (obnoxiously large ones send the most drastic signal; noise-cancelling ones are the most useful), a closed office door, going to a quiet location, hiring a babysitter, etc. Mental blinders are much harder to apply, but can be anything from sheer mental willpower to techniques that fake willpower, and will be discussed shortly.

Make It Happen: We'll talk about some more specific ideas for exactly how to make it happen in the next chapter. For now, all you need to know is that this step is the hardest, but also the simplest in reality. Making it happen is how you make it happen. Yes, there are techniques you can use to speed up the process, focus your brain, and knock things off your to-do list. But techniques are only the means to the end. The end result is making it happen. So gird those loins (whatever that means), and make. it. happen.

Work ON Your Goal, Not in It: It's so easy to get caught up in the actual mechanics of tasks and making self-discipline work. We can get rote about things, checking the boxes and taking care of the discipline side of things. But while that steady grind works, and accomplishes things, it doesn't have much vision. We must be disciplined enough to also set aside time for the big picture. Steer the ship. Be it your home, business, or day job, this is important. You want to be in charge of the rudder, not going wherever the wind blows. If your home life schedule is feeling overwhelming, it's time to purge the calendar and refocus on what matters. If your work is stuck in a rut, it's time to brainstorm outside the checkboxes. What can propel you forward? What can you do, both big and small, to work on the next step of your life or work? Budget. Hire a new employee. Add a new superfood to your routine. Or do the opposite. Perhaps you need a loan, perhaps you need to let someone go, perhaps you need to say good-bye to running because your priorities have changed. Working on your goal helps intensify your self-discipline efforts because they won't get stale. You'll be recharged and energized.

Now, When Dabbling Is Good

Of course, you have to know the rules to break them. The rule is don't dabble. But dabbling, occasionally, can be good for the spirit. Good for the mental space, a little shaking-up of things with play. Play is an intellectual exercise and good for those of us seeking self-discipline. We need to remind ourselves to occasionally dabble. To occasionally be beginners again.

Hobby Vs. Dabbling: A hobby and a dabble are two totally different things. A good old-fashioned hobby is not a dabble. A hobby must always remain fully focused on remaining a hobby (at least until your full-time hustle is no longer full-time), must always maintain amateur status, must always remain something we are interested in. A hobby is solely for pleasure, and practiced in our free time. Those are the key words: pleasure and free time. When we take a hobby to a full-time hustle, it loses its luster. I'm not sure how, but it does. When play becomes work, it is no longer fun. It is no longer as curiosity-driven. It is no longer as good for the spirit, and then it leaves us with no creative outlet. Make no mistake, I am a fan of the hobby. The hobby is an excellent tool for developing self-discipline and creative capital. But it must be done outside the confines of the hustle goal. It must be done only when all that's left to be done is done and there is downtime.

A dabble, however, is a side project done during your hustle time. Maybe you were looking at real estate for your own business, enjoyed the prospect, and started offering to find real estate for friends. Maybe you're a writer like me but you love coffee, so you spend days researching how to create your own blend of coffee to sell. Perhaps you work a 9–5, but you've found yourself on every subcommittee that ever meets. These are dabbles. Dabbles takes away from the hustle. It usurps your focus and patience. It actually drains your creative capital. What does a dabble give back? Not enough. A dabble does not give back in equal measure to what it takes. And it takes-takes-takes. Dabbles are fun for a little while. They may give us a surge of adrenaline that we're missing in our hustle grind. But make no mistake, dabbles are foes. The surge of adrenaline is focused only on the dabble's interests, not the hustle's, and while the dabble flourishes and you feel revived, the revival is focused on the dabble, and the hustle suffers even more. Do you see how this is a dangerous cycle?

Hobby on, my friend. But dabble-don't. You need every gram of your precious vital energy for changing the world. And a dabbler never changed the world.

TECHNIQUES OR TORTURE? BEATING OURSELVES INTO SUBMISSION

....

This is what most people think of when they think of self-discipline. They want techniques. They want answers. They want a quick-fix to being the most accomplished world-changer there ever was. Techniques are only tools, though, so keep that in mind. And you can't build much with just tools. You have to have knowledge, so knowledge is really the key. If you don't know how a building goes together, all of the fancy equipment in the world won't help you. You might be able to get a rudimentary dwelling up, but chances are it won't match the expectations in your head. The same is true with self-discipline.

Let me remind you again: we cannot start with techniques. Techniques are an intermediate step. Techniques are only useful when the foundation is firm. I think you're ready. You've made a goal, you've honed your hustle, you've ditched your dabble.

But what's the difference between self-discipline technique and self-discipline torture? Part of it depends on your mindset. The other part depends on your reality. The mindset quotient is easy to overcome . . . it's only torture if you believe it is. Tell your feeble mind it's a technique and keep going.

Build the mind muscle. And the reality? Sometimes things just do.not.work for us. Since we are being our own keepers, we should be able to recognize when we need to push through and when we need to push pause. Every technique is not for everybody. You develop your own series of techniques and tricks that work for you, your own self-discipline program.

Of course, being organized is one of the biggest tools for being self-disciplined. A self-disciplined life can't be sidelined by not being able to find the containers for food prep, the weight-lifting gloves for a workout, the paperwork for a big job, or the notes you took for the next screenplay. Organize, organize, organize. Label, label, label. Let me tell you a secret: Piles do *not* equal organization. Trust me, my creative brain loves to think that piles are organized chaos. It loves to think that, until I spill papers over my entire office floor looking for that parking ticket I put *somewhere* after that one business trip. Piles are chaos. Repeat after me: Piles are chaos.

If organization just isn't in your DNA, call a professional. Hire someone to organize your life and your space. Organizational professionals *live* for finding systems that work for you. They know how many years you need to keep of tax documents and how to organize them so they're out of your way. They know how to tackle the self-employment receipt-explosion-drawer. Label makers are their love language. It's extraordinary, and well worth the money. Invest in your future.

Another way you can invest in your future? Hire someone to keep the office or house tidy. You have *no* idea how much mind space this will free up for you. I guarantee it. It might take a while for you to let go of the idea of letting someone rifle through your personal space, but remember it is their job, and again, these are people for whom cleaning is a joy. They relish tackling tile grime. The space between the countertop and the fridge? They have a tool for cleaning that. Overflowing trash cans no more! Try letting go of these things so you can use your vital energy for even more amazing things.

Now that you're organized and tidy, you can sit down at your clear desk, open an organized drawer, and find everything you need to make a to-do list. Here are some specific things to try:

Opening and Closing Procedures: This is a favorite of mine, and my usual way to start and end the day. When I managed a store, we had printed checklists of the opening procedures in the morning and the closing procedures at night. I've adapted this to my morning and evening routine at home, as well as my opening and closing procedures for my writing studio (even though it's just me working there). I create an "opening procedures" checklist, with actual checkboxes because I love paper, but you can also do this on your phone or a whiteboard. Add everything that needs to be done first thing in the morning, or first when you get to the office, and be specific. Be detailed. Add brushing your teeth if you love some easy checkmarks. Do the same for the end of the day.

Take a Bite of the Elephant: I'm sure you know the joke, "How do you eat an elephant? One bite at a time!" It's silly, but it's also great self-discipline advice. Every day, take a big ol' bite of the elephant. You know, that big-big task you've got on the horizon that seems overwhelming when you look at the whole? It will remain overwhelming, and undone, until you start taking some bites. Make a call. Write an email. I'm pretty sure they give free t-shirts to anyone who eats the entire elephant, so go all out, get that t-shirt, and frame it. Or, you know, the Oscar, the big client, the big certification . . . you got this.

Swallow the Frog: The old adage of swallowing a frog first thing in the morning is a good one for self-discipline. This basically means, tackle your most difficult task first thing in the morning. Get it out of the way. You'll have your most vital energy then. If you've eaten a proper breakfast, your self-discipline brain power is at its peak. Do the one thing you don't want to do. The rest of your day should flow easily, because you've swallowed your slippery, slimy, noisy frog.

Set the Stage: Some projects have a certain personality they exude. Some are messy, some are rigid, some are elusive, some are sharp, some are shallow. Assess these intangible aspects of your goal or project. See what they need. Listen to what it tells you it wants. Finesse the situation as best you can to take into account these quirks. If you're confused by what I mean by this, just try it. See what you find when you think of a project as an entity apart from the known aspects.

Pomodoro Timer/Technique: I'm not sure why this self-discipline technique is named after an Italian tomato, but they didn't ask me, so that's what it is. The Pomodoro Timer is especially useful when you have a lot of tasks to accomplish in limited time. The time-management technique involves setting a timer for a certain amount of time (10 minutes or 25 minutes, usually), during which you focus entirely on one task. Then, you take the remaining time of the session (5 minutes to make an even 15- or 30-minute period) to take a break. Once you've completed several rounds of this technique, you take a full-session amount break. It's amazing what you can accomplish when you know a timer is about to go off.

Pareto Principle: The Pareto Principle states that 20 percent of the tasks accomplish 80 percent of the results. This means if you put in a bit of work ahead of time to work out which tasks are those 20 percent, you can do them first and make the most of your time. This is a hard one for me. I like to do the pretty, finishing-touch things first. *Then* I'll do the bulk of the work. My theory is that if I don't do the finishing-touch things first, they never happen, but when there's a deadline, the bulk of the work always gets done because it simply must. This results in plenty of style over substance, which is not the ideal self-discipline result. If you like to do things backwards like me, try the Pareto Principle instead.

Mise en Place Your Life: Mise en place is a French cooking term meaning everything is "put in its place." Mise en place means you measure out all of the ingredients and have them at hand, ready to throw into the bowl at their proper time. You clean up as you go along. The work is in the preparation, making the task itself almost as if it were on autopilot. Mise en place ensures that all ingredients make it into the bowl, keeps things tidy along the way, and saves time. We can bring the same principle to our work. Keep everything you need ready and at hand. Prepare as much as possible ahead of time so the actual task can be on autopilot.

Start Before You're Ready: There will never be a perfect time, perfect place, perfect mind-set to start a project. Something about being ready makes us feel in control. But we are never actually completely in control, so why wait until we are completely ready? Now, this is not a blank check for recklessness. This is a mind-set thing. Our minds are creatures of comfort. They want to feel completely satisfied that every possible "what if" can be managed. When we trick our brains and start before we're ready, we short-circuit that thinking process and redirect our energy toward actually accomplishing our project. You can do it. So go do it. Jump and the net will appear, as they say. You become ready when you do it.

Employ Fluidity of Motion: Use your body and your actions wisely. Ration your motion and your energy. Especially ration your vital energy. Fluidity of motion and energy means grouping tasks so you can create repetition. Make it a habit that you always grab something that needs to go somewhere else when you leave a room. Respond to emails as soon as they come in so you don't have to waste energy on it twice. If you say you'll do something, do it right then (forward an email, make a phone call) to preserve the energy your brain is already using on it. Fragmented movement and thoughts take valuable energy.

The mechanics of self-discipline come down to two things, I think: tricking your mind into doing things it doesn't want to do by changing the narrative, and routinizing just about everything you possibly can. All of these techniques accomplish both of these things. The number of techniques you can find is endless, but keep in mind they are just that: techniques. Tools. Not knowledge. Not heart. Not willpower itself. There is no passion or creativity inherent in them. That's all you.

PASSION POWERS PROGRESS AND CREATIVITY IS A CYCLE: SO, PEDAL HARD

....

Self-discipline sounds stale and stark. It sounds lonely. But self-discipline is not successful without passion. Passion is the sun that progress revolves around. Self-discipline will never make any progress without passion. Passionless self-discipline is drudgery, and no one ever went above and beyond when they were drudging.

Does the passion need to be directly related to what we're focusing our self-discipline efforts on? No. We can be passionate bakers focusing our self-discipline efforts on getting through law school. We can be passionate surfers who decide our passion is enough to build a business making surfboards. We might be passionate travelers who create a unique travel bag that suits a specific need only we saw. Passion powers progress all around. Passion starts your motor, gets your emotions involved in self-discipline. Passion is pure, and it brings that purity to self-discipline.

If we aim to be successful in our self-discipline efforts, we need to be powered by our passion. Which means we need to find it if we don't have it. It seems like some of us are born with ingrained passions . . . you know, the ones who are budding Beethovens from the womb. The rest of us, well, we might need to spend a few decades defining our passion. Because passion isn't just something we *like*, it's not something that's just *okay* in our life. It's much, much more than that.

What is passion? A passion for something goes beyond enjoying it. Enjoyment is surface-level, and passion is heart-level. Passion excites our every cell, drives us to the purity of enjoyment, and it leads us to practice perfection. Purity powers progress in a way that nothing else can. In a way, passion is the opposite of self-discipline. Self-discipline is driven by a *mind-must*. Your mind says you must do it, so you do it. Passion, though, is from another kind of must . . . the soul-must. The gut-must. The soul and gut simply must do it, or you'll explode. And if you soul-and-gut-must, then you've no need for mind-must. Passion can be anything. It can be as minute as pouring the perfect latte art, or it can be as grand as finding a specific genome. Both create fervor that snowballs into practicing the craft, defining the art, being curious about every part of the process. Passion makes sure we're awake, makes sure we're *living* this one life we're given.

How to Find Passion: Passion isn't a fruit that grows on a tree (though passion fruit is, coincidentally). Passion must be discovered, unveiled, and nurtured. If you are already wholeheartedly pursuing your passion, I commend you heartily. You've either been extremely lucky or already put in the hard work. The rest of us are going to Peruse and Pursue. If you have an inkling of what your passion is, you're a step ahead of the game. If you have no idea, then you're in for some fun.

Peruse: Peruse your current interests. Make a list of your current commitments. Write down some dream skills and activities you'd love to try. Go to the library and flip through some specialty magazines. Watch a few documentaries. See what makes your heart beat a little faster. See what makes you move to the edge of your seat so you don't miss a word. What makes you grab your notepad to make notes? What makes you run home to your computer to Google the heck out of it? What makes you say that ever-wonderful, "Hmmm, I wonder . . ." Follow that wonderment.

Pursue: Once you've got your list of current and potential passions, it's time to pursue them each with all you've got for a little bit. It's best to dive into your current interests and commitments first, though it's more enticing to go for dreams first. Chances are the things we've said yes to in the past are things we want to continue saying yes to in the future, which is great passion fodder. Our passions can lose a bit of luster, to be sure, so sometimes we need to shine them up a bit. Consider this a polishing process, just taking the things you're already interested in and seeing if you can polish them a bit to passion level. But don't worry if it doesn't come up gleaming. There's no need to panic, for there are always plenty of passion potentials.

Don't panic: Sometimes we've been doing something for so long it is no longer passion, or it never was but we got roped into it and pretended. If you've truly invested your heart in each of these items for at least one strong "go" of it (day volunteering, 10,000 words written, a week on the job, whatever you decide is enough), and none of them spark true passion, it's okay. Don't panic. This time we get to go to the "dream" side of the list . . . things we've never tried our hands at but that something inside us leans toward. Watercolor art. Tour guiding. Tax preparation. Microbrewing beer. Try it. If you can, try it through a class or low-cost investment, such as a beginner's model boat kit, first. Don't spend a boatload of money on a "build your own full-size boat" kit only to find after unpacking the thing that your heart sinks and you realize this is *not* your passion, and this boat will never hold water. Perhaps you can YouTube hours of build-your-own boat tutorials, attend a meet-up of people building their own boats, make a friend and go visit their boat-making studio. Put your hands on a handmade boat and see if it stirs something in your soul. If not, then sign up for that Intro to Tax Preparation class. You haven't lost a thing, see? You've only gained, no matter how many "nos" you go through. You've gained knowledge of your self, you've gained experience, you've gained a broader view of the world, and you've gained creative capital. Tell me that's nothing.

There's another reason we might panic, though, a slightly less obvious one. Maybe you're not sure you want to like the thing that seems to be your passion. It might come with stigma from your past, or you might think you aren't worthy of it, or maybe you find you feel guilty being interested in something so small or so large. It can be hard to go against the current of social mores, or to go against a deeply-rooted belief that our family has taught us. But I believe passion is never without purpose. And if our passion comes with purpose, how can we ignore it?

I have a friend whose passion is helping women build their self-esteem through lingerie. It's not a particularly socially acceptable job. Her social media feeds are perhaps a bit outside the norm. But she is unwilling to let social uncomfortableness get in the way of her passion to help women. She models for magazines in her underwear and swimsuits to show that all shapes and sizes are beautiful. She encourages women to be comfortable in their bodies, to know that they are more than numbers on a scale or a size tag. It's important work, and I commend her for being brave enough to do it, and for inviting other women to be brave enough to bring this part of everyday life to light. She has purpose with passion, there's no doubt about it.

Take the plunge: You've found it. Congratulations! Now it's time to take the plunge. It's scary, I know. But the only way to get something done is to do it, so . . . do it. Apply for the loan. Sign up for the class. Sign on the dotted line of the contract. Swallow your fear.

Don't forget to speak confidence to your passion. Not only to speak to it, but to speak about it with confidence. This is your passion, remember, and that means it has a purpose. Speak to it with kind words, with brave, life-giving words. You have to tell your passion you are on its side. You will work for it. Then, tell the world the same. No one believes a person who whispers about their passion with vague words and a limp face. Your passion won't even believe it, and it will wilt quickly. This may be a case of "fake it till you make it." But you'll make it, you'll make it.

Creativity

I mentioned earlier that self-discipline is not its own thing—it is the sum of all the parts. Creativity is the same. It is a sum of the parts of your inner and outer adventures and dreams. It is you, plus everything you're consuming. Consuming in the sense of reading, watching, experiencing, emoting, living. Every single little bit of your life is building creativity. But just because we have the building blocks does not mean we have the thing itself, right? A stack of bricks is nothing until it is put together. And the best news is, it can be put together in an infinite array of designs. One person builds a house, another a bridge.

When we have our passion, creativity comes next. Passion and creativity are self-discipline's best friends. Creativity takes passion to the next level. It puts those bricks together in a truly unique way, because creativity is yours alone. Now, creativity is not a given. Creativity is actually much rarer these days than you might think. We have an in-stock mentality. Is it on the shelf? Have we seen it before? Great, let's grab it, or replicate it. This world moves so fast and we have so much to accomplish that taking the time to create something new is almost unheard of. That's why, as seekers of self-discipline, we must use our time wisely and give due diligence to creativity. Yes, creativity takes a bit more time. But creative, pondering, brainstorming, work-playing time is where the magic happens.

Work-play. We all know what brainstorming is, but what is work-play? It's when you have free time during the scope of your job or working day to explore possibilities related to the job. It's not a concept I've created; many large companies do it to foster microentrepreneurship. Companies realize their employees, the ones with the behind-the-scenes knowledge, are the best ones to come up with new ideas. And those employees could very well leave and start their own rival companies with better ideas. So they foster entrepreneurship within the workday, encouraging employees to iterate within the company and create for the company's sake.

We must be self-disciplined in pedaling the creativity cycle or we'll end up coasting out of control into the weeds. Passion has a way of getting carried away with itself. Passion, well, passion can be a bit blind-sighted. Passion has no self-control. Remind your passion that it is there to power your self-discipline and keep it in check.

THE MOTIVATION MYTH: MOUNTAINS, MOLEHILLS, AND MOTIVATION

....

Motivation, I want to tell you something: *I don't need you. You're nice, but . . . you're too codependent. I need my space to be self-disciplined, and you make it hard.*

Motivation is great. But motivation is also a bit of a myth. It exists, to be sure. But constant motivation is a unicorn. It doesn't exist, you guys. Motivation is a fickle friend, and therefore, when it comes to self-discipline, I classify motivation as a foe.

Self-motivation is a different animal altogether, a narwhal, if you will, because it is just as magical but it *actually exists.* To be honest with you, I did not know narwhals were real until well into my second decade. Many of us don't realize that self-motivation exists for many decades, either.

Motivation comes in three manifestations: External, Muse, and Internal.

Motivation that is external is things like: more money, a promotion, a bigger house, a corner office, a designer suit, etc. These things are reward-based and motivate us in positive and not-so-positive ways. These are not bad things to desire. But they are bad things to use as motivation because they don't have heart. They don't have story or purpose and therefore can easily lead us astray.

Muse motivation is just that. Random gifted motivation from the "muse" that makes us get up one morning and feel like conquering the world. It's the days when people say, "I want whatever you had for breakfast!" but the truth is we didn't have anything special on our bagel this morning. Motivation, given from above, just settled upon us today to give us a little extra spark. I adore this kind of motivation because it feels good, you know? But it's the kind of motivation I mention above that is a myth. When this kind of motivation finds me, I ride that mythical unicorn as long as I can before it rides off into the sunset. Because this kind of motivation always leaves.

Internal motivation, or self-motivation, is the only kind of motivation we actually have control over. Therefore, it falls under the self-discipline category of friend, and as something we must cultivate. Cultivating motivation is a great exercise because it is self-seeding. Like plants that spread their seeds for next year, and come up year after year, motivation that is cultivated throws its seeds far and wide for you.

Internal motivation may come easily for you. Internal motivation is like an internal alarm clock for life . . . it keeps ticking and you can't ignore it until you start accomplishing things. You might find yourself throwing the covers off at 5 a.m. wide-eyed and bushy-tailed, ready to eat a whole lotta bites of that elephant. For others, the idea of taking on the world is not nearly as enticing as letting it pass us by while we stay warm and cozy until 10 a.m. But you know what happens when you sleep in until 10 a.m.? You lose time. You lose life. You lose vital energy hours. So you have to find your heart-motivation.

Heart-motivation: Heart-motivation is even deeper than simple internal motivation. Heart-motivation is all about the why. The how comes later, but that getting up thing, that finding motion to create momentum thing: that's all about the heart-motivation. What motivates your heart to get up and give its all? If getting out of bed at 5 a.m. feels impossible, think about the *one* thing that would get you up. Chances are that's your heart-motivation. Maybe it's your family, and seeing them off to work and school before you begin your own day. Maybe it's a terrifying deadline that you simply can't ignore so you'd be willing to get up at 5 a.m. to have extra vital energy hours to work on it. You might have a dream, a book, a song, a building inside your mind that you simply can't rest until you see it in the world. Maybe it's coffee. If coffee is your heart-motivation (it is certainly part of mine!), that is fine. This is your reason . . . whatever motivates you to get up, get going, and get shaking the world up with your awesomeness.

How do you find out what your heart-motivation is, and hold it in a precious space? And once you do, how does this motivate self-discipline?

Holding heart-motivation is a practice, much like yoga, where you probably won't be strong or flexible enough to do it for very long when you begin. That is why we call it a practice. It takes time, diligence, and effort to create the desired outcome. When you begin anything, you start simple. Simple heart-motivation lies in reminding yourself of your reason.

Remind yourself in the morning what motivates you. Make a photo or quotation about it your phone background, make it the words on your phone alarm clock so you see them first thing, write them on your refrigerator door (well don't actually write them *on* the door, write them on something else and then stick it up on the door), tape a little sticky note to the front of your credit card or keychain. The hardest thing to do is to get our motivation from our heart to our head. That heart-head canal is a narrow one.

Once your brain starts to get it, remind it at certain times so it correlates the motivation with your efforts toward the result. Every time you write a sentence for your book, or study for your big certification exam, or make school lunches for your children, meditate on your reason. Your why. Let it permeate your being and soak into your actions. Eventually, your actions will stem from your why. This is the goal. That your heart-reason holds so much weight, that this motivation is the thing that keeps your inner north true, that you won't listen to any other voices. That you won't need the flightiness of muse motivation, and you won't need to vainly search for external motivation. You have your motivation with you, every second of every day.

This kind of motivation keeps us from turning molehills into mountains. Oh, we love to tell ourselves stories of the giant peaks in front of us, staring us down with beady eyes and dark shadows. They make for more spectacular before-and-afters, right? And we all live for a good before-and-after tale. Maybe we should try keeping things in perspective, though. Molehills aren't worth tripping over. Molehills aren't worth spending days slogging up in heavy hiking boots with searing hot sun and no water. That is self-imposed torture, not self-discipline. Keeping a molehill a molehill . . . now that's self-discipline.

There are mountains, though, I won't lie. They aren't all actually molehills. The trick is to know the difference. When you come upon a mountain, when you use heart-motivation to navigate, you have everything you need to summit. No need to hire a guide—you're the guide. You know the way, in your heart, because you know the end result.

This is the kind of motivation that keeps self-discipline on track. External motivation is a side-track. Muse motivation is the slow lane. Heart-motivation is the fast lane for the long haul.

But you still have to do the work. You still have to show up. You still have to be hands-and-head-and-heart-and-whole-self there. And that takes courage. Self-discipline desires courage. It wants courage so badly, because courage is like a B-12 injection for self-discipline. Courage gets up and goes there.

MY HEART MOTIVATION

Sketch or write about your heart motivation. What gets you out of bed in the morning? Is it family? Faith? Your dreams?

MY HEART MOTIVATION

B-12 vitamin injections are popular among the jet-set celebrity pack. But do they help us everyday self-discipline seekers? *They might, if we're low on this nutrient that helps our bodies make energy efficiently. A simple blood test can tell us if we're running on empty. Low on B-12? Likely low on energy. But it doesn't work the other way 'round, which is that if you're low on energy you need B-12. Turns out B-12 is water-soluble, so your body just rids itself of the excess, and an injection without need will just be money down the toilet. If you're low, though, a boost by monthly injection is a boon. While you can take B-12 orally, a quick poke of the needle ensures the vitamin goes straight to good use. Is it a miracle cure? No. Is it for everyone? No. Can it help? Absolutely.*

Courage is not easy. If courage were easy it wouldn't be courage. The point of courage is that it takes discipline and heart in the face of fear. The opposite of courage is cowardice. I don't think anyone sets out to be a coward in life, to lay down at the slightest whiff of difficulty, to die a little each day because you can't fulfill your dreams. Everyone thinks being a coward is the easy way out. But it's not true. Being cowardly is just as difficult as being courageous. When you're being courageous, you're saying yes to your dreams and no to your fears. Being cowardly means saying no to your dreams, which is a very tough thing to do. It is self-sabotage, and your heart hardens a bit each time you do it.

No, no, we mustn't be cowardly, tempting as it is. Trust me, there are so many days I would prefer to stay in my safe, warm bed than go out into the world and try to hack my path to victory. Climbing mountains and maintaining mole-hills is a lot of work. We need some tools. Some metaphorical path-clearing tools.

Shovel: Ah, a shovel. The shovel is the workhorse of hand tools, as it removes things and adds things with equal ease. A shovel helps clear the earth in your path and helps fill in gaps where you need solid earth to cross. What is a shovel in this context? It's your physical strength. Your physical strength helps you remove and add things with ease.

Sieve: Sieves for dirt are large wooden frames with a screen at the bottom. Sometimes they're used to search for gold and gems. But most of the time, they're simply used to get rocks out of dirt. We all need to get some rocks out of our dirt, and sometimes we need to search for gold, too, so this is a useful tool. A sieve in our metaphor is your mindset. Your mindset helps you sift the good and bad. Throw out rocks, treasure the gemstones.

Weed Popper: This tiny little spade-shaped tool is designed to get dandelion roots up. They are known for being stubborn and deep, and they *love* to grow in crevices where getting at them with hands or a shovel would be impossible. I cannot live without this gardening tool, and likewise, I can't deal with molehills in my life without my metaphorical one. A metaphorical weed popper is a well-honed awareness. Keep your perspective and pop the weeds.

Scythe: A scythe helps you clear large swaths of land. It takes down all the grass in your way, clearing a large path for the future. These things are big, they're dangerous, and they take a skilled operator to use them in a safe and effective way. But once you manage the scythe, it's an invaluable tool. Sometimes we need to slash and burn in our lives, and this is the tool for that. Metaphorically, it's your strongest "hell no" when things get tough. This is mental fortitude to make sweeping changes in your life.

With these tools, you're well on your way to climbing mountains like a pro, keeping molehills in check, and making sure your motivation is here to stay.

SO LONG SUNDAY BLUES:
PUT ON YOUR DANCING SHOES

....

The Sunday blues are a real thing. Most of us get sad when the weekend comes to an end because demands will be heavy on our time again. Deadlines, work conflicts . . . the daily grind can have us grinding our teeth on Sunday night. But we don't need to lose a good portion of our weekend by worrying what the week will bring. The week will come, and bring with it what it brings, and it shouldn't ruin our Sunday night.

Truth is, if we have the Sunday blues, maybe our self-discipline stamina is running low. When our stamina is high, our heart-motivation is solid, and our goals are locked in, we should go to bed on Sunday night excited to spend another week working toward our dreams. Sunday should be a time to put on our dancing shoes because we get another go on the dance floor come Monday. But that isn't always reality. It is sad that the weekend is over—free time will take a back seat to hustle for the next five days. But that is good. That is the way it should be. Life is a cycle, and the work week is one too for a reason. It's tough to be our absolute best without some down time to recharge our vital energy. I have worked 7 days a week before, 12+ hour days. That is the fast-track to burnout.

Work is important, but there is also life to be lived. Laundry to be done. Loved ones to spend time with. We must know how to take our self-discipline less seriously on the weekends.

Did I just tell you to take self-discipline less seriously? Yes, I did. Not not-seriously-at-all. Just a little less seriously. Make your weekend routine a bit more flexible, because this is downtime. This is creative-capital gathering time and vital-energy gathering time. So perhaps your two pieces of toast and half a grapefruit breakfast could be changed up. Maybe it's eggs with goat cheese and chives (which takes about 5 more minutes to make but feels entirely luxurious). Instead of your usual solo gym session, you take a long bike ride with your family after dinner. Set your alarm for 6 a.m. instead of 5 a.m. Small things, little indulgences that you can savor.

Don't suddenly sleep in until 11, then eat a giant stack of waffles smothered in butter, maple syrup, and whipped cream simply because it's the weekend. This is not *off*time, just downtime. Going to "offtime" will certainly give you the Sunday blues. This is too big of a switch for our bodies and minds. We cannot suddenly throw self-discipline to the curb two days a week and expect to pick it up on Monday morning and dust it off and have it be just fine. It doesn't work that way. Self-discipline is not an on-off thing. It has different levels, though, so simply turn it down on the weekends and enjoy your life. Self-discipline is worth nothing if we aren't also living our lives.

Let Yourself Exist

Self-awareness and self-esteem are two main goals of any self-discipline journey. Believe it or not, these are accomplished in downtime. I know, you don't believe me. You think self-awareness and self-esteem are built on gridirons and concert stages, 4H banquets and trophy ceremonies. I disagree. Those things teach us what it feels like to accomplish things because of our self-awareness and self-esteem. But if they are left unchecked, those accomplishments will only build an inflated sense of self-awareness and a self-esteem linked only to accomplishment. That is not healthy.

To build healthy, life-giving self-awareness and self-esteem, we must let ourselves exist. We must relax. We must allow ourselves to take up the space we need, deserve, crave. We must ground ourselves, give ourselves roots that let us grow stronger. Wiggle into the world a little bit, shake off expectation, be here, and be happy with who you are when you're here. That's the good stuff.

Tackle the To-Dos

The world moves fast Monday through Friday, and so do we. Saturday brings obligations, be it grocery shopping, house repair, baby showers, Little League games, or all four plus more. Saturday is for the basics to be replenished, the ducks of daily life all tidied in a row and dusted off for next week, and for calling grandmas. Grandmas should always be called. Or better yet, visited. But the obligations of Saturday should not overwhelm. Use your self-discipline techniques for getting everything accomplished, too. Going to Walmart for a giant restock of life necessities is a great idea earllllllyyyy on Saturday morning or late on Saturday night. Not such a great idea at 2 p.m., when there are families with children who haven't napped crying in carriages, busy people who haven't eaten lunch yet and are hangry, and every other manner of potentially distressing scenario.

Every life has the "must-dos," regardless of your current life situation. If it isn't taking the kids to every activity imaginable, it's hauling laundry to the laundromat and trying to stock the freezer with enough frozen dinners to get you through the week. The living of life is demanding, and it takes time and effort to take care of these things. Even if we have someone to help with the laundry and the cleaning, there are things that require our presence. Church events, school events, friend and family celebrations, and our children's activities are still things we wouldn't want to miss. But they do take energy, and they do take time. Accept this. Accept it so you can be fully present while you're there. Even if you need to make a time limit and set an alarm so you can get on to the next item on the agenda, don't give away your game. Be present while you're present. Being busy is not a badge of honor, nor a badge of courage. It just makes you look busy, and perhaps even *better-than* because you have more important things to do than be there. Make a graceful exit when you must, and be sure to say good-bye. No phantom-ghosting allowed, no matter how much you have to do.

Tackle Saturday with fervor. Get everything accomplished. But keep some margins on the edge for fun. Fun, ahhh, yes, that oft-neglected piece of the puzzle. You may think you don't have time for fun. You may not want to make time for fun. But fun is healthy for you. Fun shakes up your neurons and releases endorphins. Including fun in your weekend routine will likely make you a better human being in general, so get those dancing shoes on! Grab a drink with a friend, see a film in the theater instead of on your computer, get a babysitter and go to a concert with your loved one.

Fun also helps you blow off steam and get rid of that distress that might be lurking from the past week or rearing its head for the upcoming week. Fun helps build self-esteem, believe it or not. Self-esteem thrives when there is fun to be had, and life isn't entirely run on scores, accomplishments, and "doing things right." Play makes a bit of fun of self-discipline, which is something I love.

It's hard to hold distress and fun at the same time, and fun takes priority on the weekends. Play keeps you well-rounded. Invest in the world and you'll be rewarded with creative capital. When you get back to the office, you'll find yourself less afraid to take risks. You'll find yourself looking at things from new perspectives and coming up with creative solutions.

Ideas for Fun: *Go to a museum, be a tourist in your own town, get ice cream at a local diner, ride your bike, row your boat/kayak/canoe, go fishing, attend a random event in your town (mine has a BaconFest, you know I'll be there!), participate in a 5K, go for a hike, go camping, take a day trip, complete a project around*

the house, send all of the mail and packages that have been piling up, try something totally adventurous like rock climbing or zip-lining.

Sunday . . . ahhhh, Sunday. The Sabbath day of rest for millennia is still our breath of air in the week. Sunday is the best time to refuel your self-discipline stamina by taking on some self-care rituals.

Fun is all about pleasure, in an active sense. Self-care is about pleasure in a restorative, peaceful sense. Active relaxation. Do things that relax you *and* make you feel good about yourself. The *and* is key there, as the activities must do both. No binge-eating ice cream and watching Netflix until your eyes are stuck open. How about a fresh manicure while you watch a documentary? And I won't say no to a glass of wine.

A self-care routine is a great way to make sure you follow through, and the self-discipline junkie in you will love it. You can even have a checklist if you like. A bath, a shower, a shave, a haircut, all of those little luxurious grooming things we don't necessarily get to every day of the week are good self-care fodder. So are larger self-care things, like steams, saunas, or massages. These are investments in your body, which is your main self-discipline instrument, and it's the only one you have. Treat it well.

Ideas for Self-Care: *Get a membership to a local pool that also has a sauna/steam room, take a long afternoon nap in the sunshine, bake, brew up some herbal tea, read a book for pleasure, go shopping for new clothing (this can totally be self-care, believe me), go to the farmer's market and cook up something fresh and tasty, sit on the porch and think about nothing, call your parents, write a letter or postcard to a friend, simply put your feet up (on the coffee table, cooler, porch railing, anything) and take a deep breath.*

MY IDEAS FOR SELF-CARE

List some ways you can care for yourself. Then, if it's not something you can do right away, write down when you will do it and stick to that date or time.

_____

_____

_____

_____

_____

_____

_____

_____

_____

_____

_____

_____

_____

_____

_____

_____

_____

_____

_____

_____

_____

You'll also want to use some time on Sunday to put your week in order. It is imperative to start the week with a clean slate, so finish any pesky tasks around the house that are taking up space in your brain. If you can't finish them, at least write them down somewhere you'll see them. Make a list of everything you would like to accomplish this week, to get it out of your brain and onto paper.

If it isn't on paper, it's taking up mental "data," which are in limited supply. Write it down. Lara Casey, a mama of three who created something called Powersheets, calls this the "download" before the week. Simplify your life by getting it out of your brain and onto paper, be it your planner, the family calendar, a bullet journal, or the to-do list magnet on the fridge. Just make sure you'll be able to find it again.

Plan meals and prep lunches. Wash or cut up fruit so it can easily be eaten or thrown in a lunch bag. Put away the groceries from the week, change the trash, run the dishwasher. Plan outfits, iron shirts, put away the laundry, and change the sheets (this always makes the week feel fresh to me). Those are my nonnegotiables on Sunday if they haven't been done already during the free moments of Saturday. As I said earlier, *mise en place* your life. Simplify, simplify, simplify! The week is much more manageable when my mind is free and my house is tidy.

THE CRASH-AND-BURNOUT: AVOID AT ALL COSTS

....

Did you know there are actually two kinds of stress? Distress, which is what most of think when we say "stress" and Eustress, which is, believe it or not, a good kind of stress.

Eustress: Positive Stress

Positive stress keeps us on our toes. It motivates us to do our best, helps us want to get on the stage even though distress courses through our bodies and says no, makes us stay with self-discipline when we want to give up. Eustress is a normal amount of nerves that kicks our adrenaline into gear and makes things happen. Self-discipline loves to see things happen. Eustress is healthy, when it remains at a healthy level.

Eustress can also be a sign of good old-fashioned fun. The weekend is a good time to practice our eustress and keep it in good working order. Examples of eustress include the feeling as you wait in line before running your first 5K; the nerves of attempting to bake your first-ever macarons, a notoriously tricky French pastry; staring down the three-story water slide with your children; taking the shovel to the ground to start building an addition to your family house.

These things get the stomach butterflies working. But this time, it's anticipation. It's excitement. Letting your body know that these feelings are not related directly to work or distressing situations is important. Our bodies learn from us. So we tell the body: This is good, this is fun, this is normal, and these butterflies mean I am about to embark on something new and challenging.

It is important to let these feelings remain normal, to remain a part of our lives that we manage well. If we get in our heads that stomach butterflies mean we should run and hide because we are in distress, well, we're headed for disaster.

Our guts are connected to our brains; in fact, many scientists call the gut the second brain. Tending our guts well means tending our brains well. A healthy brain-gut connection is necessary for self-discipline because it combines our instincts and our intellect, creating an unstoppable combination of knowledge of one's self.

But how does one tend to a gut? Well, first of all, we have to realize what our gut is, what its role is, and how to listen to it.

The gut is technically your entire gastrointestinal tract, which starts at your mouth and ends at . . . well, your bottom. When you get anxious, sometimes your stomach feels like it rises into your throat, the butterflies start going crazy, you feel like you couldn't swallow your food even if you wanted to, and so forth. Your entire gastrointestinal tract reacts to what's happening in your brain. But really, the thing we talk about most when we mean your gut is the literal feeling in your stomach, and the way your brain interprets that feeling.

The gut knows what the heart and brain have trouble articulating. It is a more primal response, more deeply rooted than we are conscious of because this feeling is an unconscious one. We cannot make our gut feel a certain way about a situation. If a situation feels dangerous, no amount of logic will make that feeling in our stomach go away. As such, it is a very reliable indicator and often speaks truth to our bodies before our brains know what is happening.

If you've never paid any attention to your gut, other than a basic "food in, food out" philosophy, it's time to learn to listen. You have to train yourself to listen, so begin by sitting still and quietly. Focus your attention on your belly. Let your mind be at ease and quiet all of the distracting thoughts that tend to flood in. Breathe deeply into your belly. Become aware of how it feels when it is well-fed, happy, being breathed into, and relaxed. This is your base-line. Your happy-belly. Now, think of something that makes you very excited (an upcoming trip, big work commendation, your wedding, etc.) and feel it in your stomach. Chances are you'll feel a quickening of sorts, a bit of butterflies and a lovely little happiness existing there. Now, try thinking of something sad or scary, such as a loved one's passing, a time you failed a big test, etc. Your stomach will follow suit and become a bit heavier, a bit more hollow-feeling. The butterflies turn to a tightening, and you might even find yourself shaking your head, too.

Now that you can tell the feelings on their own, you'll need to pay attention to them during your daily life. Your stomach plays offense and defense. That gut feeling is offense. It lets you know ahead of time something is good or bad so you can react accordingly. Sometimes it plays defense, reacting to your actions and trying to get you to change course. Of course, it's best to have strong offense and only play defense when that fails.

The truth is, your gut instinct is rarely wrong. In fact, I'm not sure it's ever wrong, because it is, as I mentioned, a form of preconsciousness. Bodies know best.

What are some things your body knows best? When you need to push through and when you need to take a break. Guts are great at telling us when to take care of ourselves. Guts are also great at telling us when to take risks and when to wait. Guts love to tell us when people and relationships are bad fits for us, and guts also love to act as ringing egg timers on just about anything in our lives . . . time to move, time to change jobs, time to go to the doctor. Guts are also the first sign of distress.

Distress

Distress happens when stress in our lives (or any small part of it) gets out of control. That means we literally lose control over the stress in our lives and it controls us. Distressing situations can happen no matter how self-disciplined we are. Life has a way of loving to challenge us with curve balls and dead ends. But self-discipline never lets distress end in destruction.

Work is a major source of distress in our lives. Deadlines loom, interpersonal communications are tough, customers take out their anger on us, bosses demand better than our best. Then there's financial distress: the bills pile up faster than the paychecks come in, and one unexpected setback can be disaster. Relationships cause distress if they're strained. The truth is, while these three are major stressors, just about anything in our lives can become distressing.

Self-disciplined individuals can actually be more susceptible to distress. We are more susceptible because we hold ourselves to high standards. Meeting our high standards is just not always possible under the pressures of life. This is why we must be disciplined in managing distress so it does not become burnout.

While a doctor can measure cortisol (the "stresshormone") levels, you can also tell how well you're doing by being quiet inside yourself for a moment. Assess the current situation in your body. How is it reacting to the world around you? Is your stomach or lower back tight? Your jaw clenched? Your neck stiff? Are your shoulders up around your ears? Distress is taking over. Time to stretch, relax all of your muscles, and take deep breaths. Lower those cortisol levels. Take a walk outside, play with a child or dog, shake off the distress.

Managing Stress

We don't want to completely lose our eustress when we try to negate distress. It must stay in its proper place. Make a plan to keep it in its proper place, no more, no less. Know your own "line" and when you're about to cross it. Know what helps when you're about to cross it. And know what to do when you've gone waaaay past the line, because it happens to the best of us.

Look to the past to learn how you've responded before and to evaluate whether or not those coping mechanisms worked.

MY CRISIS STORY

Write about a time when you crashed and burned. Who got hurt? How did things get to that point? What could you have done differently?

_____

_____

_____

_____

_____

_____

_____

_____

_____

_____

_____

_____

_____

_____

_____

_____

_____

_____

_____

_____

_____

_____

Identify a time in your life when your distress reached a crisis level. Write down the story of what happened, both externally and internally. Evaluate the situation with hindsight and compassion. Did you hurt others in the process of trying to cope? Did you hurt yourself? How, specifically? What were the main problems?

Now that you can see the issues, you can address them during smaller distressful situations. If hurting others is the main issue, learn how to manage that. Saying to a partner, "I'm feeling completely overwhelmed right now," is the best place to start. Let them know that your coping mechanisms are failing and you feel up to your neck in responsibility. This gives them the truth, a chance to help, and also a reason that is neutral (not directed at them) for your distress. Most partners appreciate simply being told the truth instead of left to guess what's getting your goat. Then listen to your gut. Do you need to accept their offer of help? Do you need to suggest a way they can help you that they didn't think of? Or do you need to take a nap and shake it off? Take care of yourself instead of hurting others when you feel overwhelmed.

Maybe you turn to dangerous vices. We all have our vices. Vices help us through tough times, and that's fine. They are not all bad and can be useful. Of course, it is best to have good vices, such as exercising, cleaning, or investing yourself in personal projects. But it takes self-discipline to get there. I would like to say this, though: Vices are choices. I am not talking about addictions, but simply things we turn to during periods of difficulty. We must make friends with positive choices. Mine, I kid you not, is going to thrift stores and hunting for treasures. For some reason thrifting through racks of junk searching for gold is a great metaphor for tough times in life, and I find some gems along the way. There are no expectations at the thrift store; no pressures, no guilt, and no regret. And the prices don't break the bank. That's a pretty good vice if I may so myself, but perhaps the same cannot be said for my second-favorite vice: eating ice cream. Nightly. With hot fudge. And whipped cream. You only live once, though, you know?

Perhaps distress is an instant "off" switch for you, and your body and mind shut down with a depressing noise and a glaringly blank screen. Of course, this is detrimental to self-discipline because when we are so overwhelmed we can't function at all, we accomplish nothing, which only fuels overwhelm. This reaction, another one I am familiar with, makes me sad, because when we shut off our minds and bodies, we also miss all of the joy in our lives. You can't shut off just one emotion, so we end up turning them all off to get "overwhelm" off. Fighting this auto-off mechanism is tough, but it is necessary. Hard times are impossible to escape in real life, so we must deal with them. Or they will deal with us, and hard times never tread lightly.

Truth is, our self-discipline means that our coping mechanisms and vices absolutely must be constructive. There is simply no room for toeing the line of addiction or destruction. At the very-very least, they must be neutral. This is a whatever-it-takes situation. Vices and coping mechanisms-gone-wrong are a surefire way to crash and burn in a fast and hot flame. You will go down, and it won't be pretty.

When your body is hyped on adrenaline, many of us are drawn to exercise to "get it out" and exhaust that adrenaline.

I prefer the opposite. I avoid vigorous exercise when I'm stressed, because it simply adds to my adrenaline rush, stresses my body further, and raises my cortisol levels. I go for gentle things . . . centering, balancing activities that turn *off* the adrenaline pump instead of simply exhausting it. Adrenaline is useful when you're feeling overwhelmed, because sometimes you need to power through, so I prefer to reserve it for when I need it rather than arbitrarily empty it.

Centering, balancing things varies for each of us, but breathing is universal. It forces your body to slow down and focus on something necessary, rather than on stressing over unnecessary things. To immediately stop stress, try a 5-5-5 breathing technique. Breathe in for 5 seconds, hold it for 5 seconds, and breathe out for 5 seconds. Repeat the cycle until you feel calmer. Then go into a 10–10 breathing pattern, breathing in for 10 seconds and breathing out for 10 seconds. After the immediate calm down, this brings the breath into center again. Do this in your office chair, in the car, before bed at night, before getting out of bed in the morning . . . really, this can be done anywhere, anytime.

Gentle exercise, is, of course, helpful. Things such as stretching, yoga, pilates, and slow, long walks are all ideal. I also love my Prana mat, a therapeutic massage mat, which creates a stimulation similar to acupressure. The mat is thick coconut fiber, topped with a cover that features sharp plastic lotus flowers where each petal of the hundreds of flowers puts gentle pressure on the skin and releases stress. Start with 20 minutes lying on the mat while wearing a medium-weight shirt (trust me, don't go straight to bare skin). Use a pillow under your head to keep your neck in alignment and cover yourself with a blanket to keep warm. I also enjoy a hot water bottle placed on my chest or stomach to stay warm and add a calming presence. If you have a gravity blanket, that would be ideal here, as well. Work up to 45 minutes on the mat and remove items of clothing as you become more comfortable with the sensation.

Granted, many of these things take time. And time is, of course, often in short supply when we are feeling distressed. But taking time to calm yourself gives you back more efficiency and clarity. If you really can't afford 20 minutes of gentle yoga, you'll have to fake it. Dab a few drops of essential oil of peppermint (for alertness), lavender (for calmness), or lemongrass (for inspiration) on your pulse points. These wake up your central nervous system and have an aromatherapy effect that works instantly.

If you do crash and burn, you're in for a recovery period. It's much, much better to avoid burnout in the first place, because recovery is a slow process. When you crash and burn, the smoke takes a while to clear, and you may have burned a few things beyond recognition in the process.

Some commitments, relationships, and projects will not survive. That is okay, but it does require a bit of patching-up of the situation, followed by a mourning period. When you miss deadlines, flake on showing up to important presentations or meetings, or totally bail on commitments, you'll have some explaining to do. Tell the truth. This is no time to sugarcoat things, because no one likes someone who doesn't show up and then lies about the reason. Simply say, "I am so sorry I messed this up. I was overwhelmed and simply wasn't able to follow through, as much as I wanted to."

This may not be enough for some, but it has to be enough for you, because it is the truth. If they cannot understand this, they may not be people you want in your life. Overwhelm and crash-and-burn happens to the best of us. None of us intend it to happen, or want it to happen. If they let you go because of your infraction, wish them the best, and be on your way. If you were so overwhelmed you missed showing up, I think you can let something from your plate drop. They've just decided for you, they're the thing you drop. Swallow your pride and take it with courage. Then take a nap, and take a few minutes to cry if you need to. This won't feel good. No, it won't, and you are allowed to react to that.

When you've made amends (or taken your leave) from the commitments that you accidentally didn't fulfil, it's time to take stock and take a break.

Take Stock: You are obviously overscheduled, overworked, overcommitted. Write down everything you do in a day/week/ month. Be honest. You may think the 1-hour a week meetings you attend aren't worth writing down. But a 1-hour meeting requires at least 2 hours of brain power (prep time, travel time, lost time switching tasks) and must be accounted for. Be realistic with how long activities take you, not how long you wish they took you, or how long they take you on your best, most productive day. That isn't fair (but it sure is a bonus when it happens!). List it all, breathe a sigh of relief at having it all down on paper, and then take a nap if you can. Seriously, close

TIME INVENTORY

Day	Activity	Amount of Time
Sunday		
Monday		
Tuesday		
Wednesday		
Thursday		
Friday		
Saturday		

your eyes for even five minutes. Listing your time-sucks is emotionally draining and chances are, if you've crashed and burned, your list is overwhelming.

Take a Break: You need a break. You are worth it. Crashing and burning serves no one, so you need to step back until you are able to serve again. You may need a short break or a long break. If you've crashed and burned, chances are you'll need at least a medium break. If you gamble on a short break, there's no telling if the work you've done will stick, or if you'll relapse into another crash and burn. Best to break once, rather than break down twice. This is hard for those of us who crave self-discipline. But once again, self-discipline takes many forms, and forcing yourself to take a necessary break is one of those forms. It is hard to do. Therefore, we must discipline ourselves to do it.

Taking a break may mean taking a sabbatical from work. Or you may need to send the kids to Grandma's house for a week. You may need to rent a hotel room and get some peace and quiet for a weekend. Try not to make your break permanent at this stage. That is, don't quit your job *yet.* Don't consult the divorce lawyer *yet.* You need to be healthy and calm when you make those sorts of decisions, and a good break sure helps. Don't worry, if those things are nagging at you deep down, you'll get the chance to make it happen.

Free Up Time: Now you have to do some life triage. Not everything can demand all of your attention. Whittle it down. There are too many things on your list. Or maybe there is just one too many, but this one thing is a huge time and vital-energy suck and you must let it go. Be honest with yourself. Listen to your gut. Be brave. Let it go. Let me tell you something: When you let something go, it's scary at first. And then it becomes freeing. You free up mind-space. You free up time-space. You free up your vital energy and you free up *you*. That's totally worth it. Let go of the things that are no longer good for you.

Make a Move: Now is the time to make the big move. You have some free time and you're healthy. You're feeling strong, so go big. Play your cards. Ask for a raise because you're working way beyond the scope of your job. Sign your kids up for daycare once a week so you can hustle harder. Commission the artwork for your next book so you can focus on the words. Book the trip to England because it feels right. Upgrade to the fancy equipment so you can uplevel your game and leave frustration with old equipment behind. You know what your move is. Make it.

Bounce Back: Crashing and burning is serious. It takes time to bounce back. Letting something go will bring relief, but it is not a cure. Making a move is medicine, but not a cure. You can take a break, make a move, and still find yourself on the edge of the fire. You must simultaneously bounce back. Of course, this means going back to your basics. Always back to your basics! Then, take it slowly. Ration your vital energy. Feed your vital energy well, with passion and creativity and with loving care. You've learned a lesson through this crash-and-burn scenario, I hope. Tuck that lesson in your heart, carry it over your head, wear it on your sleeve. You got this.

TRUTH AND VIRTUES: THE TRUTH IS, VIRTUE IS GOOD FOR YOU

....

Virtue is a bitter pill to swallow sometimes. We don't like it nowadays, because being virtuous has essentially no meaning anymore. Truth is the same way . . . truth is no longer true, it seems. We've made truth relative. Your truth is *your* truth . . . but if everyone's beliefs are true, then is anything true? Anything, and everything, goes these days.

The trouble with this theory is that logic says conflicting "truths" cannot both be absolutely true. Not your truth. Not my truth. If we are convinced everything is true, we've actually lost truth. Only some things can be true. Only some things can be virtuous. There is no light without dark, no wet without dry. Without both, neither exists. I think we can agree we live in a world where evil exists. That must mean somewhere, somehow, something is actually truly true and good and righteous.

So amidst all of this moral chaos, why bother being persistent, patient, virtuous? Why search for real truth, be truthful, or admire truthfulness? Why bother being ethical and good, doing the right thing even when nobody is watching? And what does this have to do with self-discipline?

Truth is, virtues do still exist, whether we acknowledge them or not. Universal truths still exist. Our acknowledgement or disregard of them does not change their truthfulness. There are some things that stand the test of time, that reside deep in our beings as ethical or unethical, good or bad. Doing harm to others? Bad. Persistence? Good. Patience? Tough, but good. Empathy? Worth it.

So why should we go against the grain? Why take a stand on virtue and truth? Why dare to try to explain the nuances of logic when even logic seems to have lost its place? Because self-discipline is only useful when it is true. It is only useful when it is passionate about taking virtue seriously.

Rock Bottom

The quest for self-discipline is a quest for truth in oneself. It is also a quest for truth in the world. This is the nature of self-discipline. We are looking to find the rock-bottom, truest-true inside ourselves . . . and to see what it is made out of. Finding rock bottom requires going to, well, rock bottom. It's never fun to hit rock bottom in your life, but I promise you it is a place worth going at least once in your life. The things it teaches you cannot be learned in any other way. Self-discipline will not be as true if you haven't seen what you're made of. We must see hitting rock bottom as a quest for truth. We must respect this. It is all part of the process, and it is good work.

What do you find when you hit rock bottom? Volcanic rock from turbulent times? Granite, hard and unyielding, cold, but beautiful? Coal, which fuels progress but is dirty to unearth? Diamond in the rough, in need of polishing? Fool's gold, perhaps. Maybe slate, a soft rock that cuts easily but is also used to protect houses and create useful things.

Just as soon as we find what our rock bottom is (in a good way), we suddenly see the need for virtue. Put another way, we suddenly see its opposite. Rock bottom has a way of showing you the ugliest part of yourself, the slimiest layer that should never see the light of day. But desperation shines the light on it. We find ourselves doing anything, *anything*, to get rid of the pain, discomfort, and fear that comes from being way down in the hole of our own rock bottom.

We must not stay there long. We mustn't. Get a ladder, get a rope, climb tooth and nail and scream your lungs out if you find yourself here for long because it is a slow death at rock bottom. We disintegrate from our former selves—good people, we thought—into animals. We steal, we fight, we look out only for #1, and our base survival instincts, our animal instincts, kick in. It. gets. ugly. No, no.

Trauma and tragedy (the basis for most rock-bottom scenarios) bring out the worst in us but require the best in us. It's this mean little game the world plays. Survival of the fittest and all that; only they don't tell you it's the survival of the grittiest, the emotionally strong, the ones who stare impossibility in the face and say, you don't scare me. Only the strongest survive with their virtues close and their truths true. The rest of us just create a mud pit, and then we wallow in it something fierce.

You know what else we'll find down there, though, if we look? We'll find strength previously unknown. We'll find resilience beyond belief. We'll find courage, compassion, empathy, creativity. We'll see how pain can have silver linings, how cloudy skies turn blue and how spring always comes, no matter what. These are the gemstones. Rubies and emeralds and opals and sapphires that we had within ourselves but we didn't know existed.

Those are the things we need for self-discipline, and we need them hard-fought and tough-won. Otherwise they are theoretical nonsense, things that well . . . *might* be nice. We *might* have time to tend them someday. The time is now, the day is now, and yes, it is quite nice, so make them happen.

Necessity is the mother of invention. And while desperation itself never made dreams fly, things that come out of desperation are ripe for dreaming and flying. Do you see the difference? When you go on a date, heaving desperation into the air between the two of you, chances are the other party will run away as fast as they can. But if you notice that desperation causes anxiety before dates and thereby hinders what could potentially be great matches, and develop a platform to help dating singles ease their anxiety: boom, something that came out of your desperation just went and flew the coop.

Virtue is a self-discipline friend. It is always there, always lending us a quiet hand, always giving us a leg up. But let's look at a few times virtue really comes into play with self-discipline.

Practicing Patience

Self-discipline seems to be about always doing something. Always moving, always running toward the goal. But what about patience? Ouch. Didn't think I'd mention that, did you? But patience is a virtue, one of those long-known truths that society seems to forget every few generations. And that I seem to forget every few minutes. Patience is necessary for self-discipline, though. We can only do so much on our ends toward making things happen. There are other factors involved, other people on the team, other variables at play. We must bide our time well.

I envy my friends who are "go with the flow" sort of personalities. I imagine their lives must be so much easier than my "control it all" personality lets mine be. Practicing patience is a lifelong effort for the rest of us. I call this "running the middle." Marathon runners are long-distance lovers, but they know all too well the slump of the middle distance. There's something about the middle that we are preconditioned to not like. We don't have the fun of beginning, nor the thrill of finishing. This is merely the toil, the in-between, the means to the end. We're running the middle. Run it well, my friends. Here is a glass of water and a banana for the long haul; or, at least, a few tips on being patient. Same thing.

Breathe: When I am impatient, the first thing I forget is my breath. I hold it all in my stomach and chest, turning it into an internal fire of rage. Immediately practice the 5-5-5 technique mentioned earlier (pg 114) to calm your inner self. Breathe in for 5 seconds, hold for 5 seconds, and breathe out for 5 seconds. Even one round of this will help calm your blood pressure.

Shake It Off: Take a walk. Stress melts when we get our bodies moving softly, so walk and leave worry behind. Literally give your shoulders a good shake. Center your body over your feet. Feel the weight of your being, the way your body carries itself. Adjust as necessary. Bring everything into alignment. Focusing on your physical body takes the onus off the things you can't control.

Change the Channel: Change the channel in your brain. We love to watch the static of waiting, even if it gives us a headache. You have power over your thoughts, so change the channel. If your waiting period is long, the best thing you can do to pass the time is distract yourself. Change your surroundings, call a friend, engage your brain in anything other than the thing requiring patience.

Talk to Someone You Love: When waiting seems interminable, talk to someone you love. Science proves that hearing a loved one's voice can calm stress.[3] Even if science told me it didn't work one iota, I wouldn't believe them, because I know it works. Familiar voices mean something to us, and they speak to us on a deeper calming level. Plus, loved ones are likely to get us to laugh, which is a bonus.

Laugh: Watch a comedy show. Watch old home videos. Play with your children, really investing in the play. Laugh down into your gut, where it really means something.

---

3   Carroll, Linda. "A Mom's Voice is Powerful Medicine." NBCNews.com. May 12, 2010. www.NBCNews.com.

Keep Going: A lot of times when our patience is running thin it's because we aren't seeing our desired results immediately. We must keep going. Keep the pace. Immediate results are mostly a myth. Things worth having are worth working for, so put in the work to see the results.

Or Quit: Maybe you really need to quit. Maybe it's time to throw in the towel. There are probably a lot of self-discipline books that will tell you to never, ever throw in the towel. That winners don't quit. False. Plenty of winners quit many things before they find the thing they are ultimately winners at. Your gut will tell you when to quit. Then start over. It is called iteration, and we iterate all our lives.

If All Else Fails, Clean: Cleaning is the fall-back plan of anyone trying to fill time and avoid the agony of simply sitting and waiting. It accomplishes something, which is good for a brain on hold. It shines something up, serves a purpose, and needs to get done anyway. Win-win-win.

Avoiding Boredom

Staying active and engaged in life is a virtue, too. It is so easy to slip into slothfulness, slovenliness, and self-loathing (the 3 S's) when we're bored with life. When I was a child, my grandpa would literally make me sit in a chair and twiddle my thumbs if I dared to say I was bored. How could I, a child with boundless imagination and energy, not find something to do? I was given something to do. Something worse than all the other things I could have been doing . . . you know, playing with the entire pile of toys right in front of me, coloring in the stack of coloring books, reading one of the numerous books on the bookshelf, playing with several neighbor children, etc. And it worked. Now, every time I am bored, I think to myself, "Find something to do or go twiddle your thumbs."

Boredom is actually laziness. It's just another word for it, sneakily wrapped up in grandiose ideas of self-pity. Laziness is so common in our culture that they've even named a chair after it . . . a chair that reclines for you and is padded, has a drink holder, a remote holder, and maybe even a miniature cooler. Society thinks so little of you and your dreams that they encourage you to embrace the three S's. They encourage you to give up. Now, giving up for one night at the end of a very rough day is one thing. I don't call that laziness, I call that resting. But laziness and boredom, that's when you have energy in your bones to do things, but your mind says, "Meh." Your mind says, "Hmm, that recliner over there looks pretty comfy to me, and, well, I haven't earned putting my feet up but it's there and my feet sure wouldn't mind being put up."

Get up. Get off your cushy bottom and do something. That's all there is to it. Do something. It doesn't matter what; anything'll do. Cut the grass, read over the flashcards one more time, try saying your presentation without your notes this time, bake a pie, ride your bike around the neighborhood. It really doesn't matter what you do or how goal-oriented it is. The idea is simply to get going. Don't waste this precious life you have being lazy. Life doesn't come to us; we have to go get it. We have to engage in it.

When we're lazy we're usually just scared. Scared that if we do something it will turn out wrong, or we'll look stupid, or maybe we haven't broken down a task into small enough parts to make it manageable. There's usually a reason for laziness, and it's usually fixable. Fix it. I know that isn't very useful advice, but it's the only advice that works. To do something, you have to do it. To make it happen, you have to make it happen. Things don't happen by accident. Nothing great ever happened without work. The universe doesn't drop bars of gold into our hands and tell us to call it a day and go inside to spend some quality time with our recliner.

Honor and Integrity

Hmmm, honor and integrity. Nitty-gritty little words there when it comes to self-discipline. Self-discipline can be seen as an at-all-costs sorta thing, principles be darned. Self-discipline must conquer all. I reject this idea. Self-discipline operates quite nicely on higher moral ground, and I might even say, it operates better. Honor and integrity are in it for the long haul. Honor and integrity treat the world like a small town; everyone knows everything, and it all comes back to you at some point or another. Reputations travel far and fast.

See, honor and integrity aren't just concerned with getting things done. They are concerned with getting things done well, and with good intentions. You cannot take your honor captive to complete the objective. Your soul will die. It may feel good at first; you may feel like a hero with no one to answer to. But a hero without a moral compass is actually a villain. We all have someone to answer to, actually: ourselves. We are accountable to ourselves because we have to fall asleep at night and hope our consciences allow us to. We have to look our children in the eyes, look our supervisors in the eyes, look ourselves in the eyes, every day. I'm not a liar; never have been, never will be. I'm terrible at it; always giving away the truth, however sordid or embarrassing.

I cannot see how self-discipline and ruthless tactics work together. Self-discipline's job is to keep the ruthlessness in check. It says, "Woah, there, buddy, are you really thinking about doing business with those unscrupulous people to accomplish your goal?" There is always another way. It may not seem like it, but there is. And 9.999-infinity times out of ten, it ends up being a better way. Self-discipline stops greed in its tracks because greed is, by definition, an excess, which is not at all self-disciplined.

Dishonesty and disrespect are everything self-discipline seeks to abandon, seeks to root out. There is no room for them, and self-discipline has no tolerance for them.

Boundaries Are Not Bad: Block Out Your Time

Boundaries are necessary for self-discipline. We simply must protect our time and vital energy. I'm not sure why we think boundaries are bad. It must be this deep-seated fear that blocking off time means blocking out other things that could be better. This is false. The grass is greener where you water it, and you can't water the entire field. Water your plot. Water it well, keep your fence painted white, and see what bounty you can produce. More than enough, I have no doubt.

The fear of blocking things out is real. We are programmed to keep options open, it seems, so choosing one means saying no to the other options. But not choosing one means saying no to all of them, really. When we haven't made a choice, we have none of the options. Choosing one means we have a plot to cultivate. And nothing grows without care.

Boundaries help us say yes. Boundaries are a good thing. Blocking out our time means we say yes to the things that matter. We prioritize and triage our lives because sometimes things get a little chaotic. Blocking out our time protects our assets and sets a firm foundation for self-discipline. If we don't have the time to devote to certain tasks, they will not get accomplished in a streamlined and stress-free manner, no matter how disciplined we are. The bulk of self-discipline comes from being disciplined with our time.

But how do we know which boundary lines to build up and which to let down?

Building Boundaries: It takes time and discipline to build good boundaries. You must build them well or they are apt to fall down. More accurately, they are apt to be taken down by others who wish to have no demands on your time but their own. This includes bosses, family, coworkers, children, etc. Everyone loves to be the only priority. But you are the one who sets your priorities. Decide what your values are. Do you value family over work? Then work needs to have more boundaries around it to protect family time. Maybe you have friends who take more than they give, and your social life needs a few boundaries. Maybe well-meaning family members keep questioning your decisions, and a few boundary lines wouldn't be remiss.

There are three stages to building boundaries, and none of them is particularly fun. It's much better to start with firm boundaries at the beginning of a situation, but we all know that isn't possible, since we don't usually have the information necessary to know where to build our boundary lines. So we get out our tripods and survey the land to gather more information.

Survey: Survey the situation. Each situation requires different information, and it must be recorded well so you can best identify how and where to set the boundaries. One important piece of information to consider is what the other person(s) involved is/are thinking. Why are they overstepping here? What is their motivation to do so? Is there a way I can help them fulfill their motivation, making the boundary unnecessary? Perhaps they are unaware of the distress they are causing you. It is unlikely that their main goal is to make you unhappy in life, so do a little empathy-sleuthing and see what you come up with. You'll also need to examine your own motives. Are you being too selfish? Are you being too harsh, too reactionary, too stiff? All of the information helps set clear boundaries that help you, not hurt you, and aim not to hurt others, either.

Gather materials: Setting up a boundary line requires a few materials. In real life, we're talking stakes, flags, and fishing line or spray paint. In this case, it might be a planner, a babysitter, a specific meeting time for team Q&A sessions to avoid constant interruptions, an interoffice messaging system to limit phone calls, etc. Don't begin to implement your bound-

MY BOUNDARIES

What boundaries do you need to set? Whom do you need to tell? How will you keep your ground?

_____

_____

_____

_____

_____

_____

_____

_____

_____

_____

_____

_____

_____

_____

_____

_____

_____

_____

_____

_____

_____

_____

ary plan until you have the necessary tools to make it happen. There's nothing worse than flimsy, unclear boundaries. People love to take advantage of those.

Set up Flags: Now you'll set up your flags, the beginning of the implementation process. Setting these little flags in the ground is penciling in the boundary. In life, this means beginning to swing the pendulum toward your boundary. If this is going to be a hard-and-fast boundary that other people need to know about, prepare them ahead of time. Start telling people the change will be happening. Give them a start date for the boundary. Prepare them so the boundary doesn't become a wall they smack their heads into hard on day one. Or, if this is a boundary that won't be announced, start inching the relationship toward it little by little. Ease those involved into the idea so it doesn't seem arbitrary to them.

Build the Boundary: Now you must follow through. You've dropped the hints, planned the date . . . now build the boundary. I find it best to be honest about the new boundary rather than trying to sneak it into place. "I am so glad you have so many questions. That's great. What we're going to do from here on out is write them down on the new giant whiteboard in the hallway and we'll discuss them each week during our Q&A sessions." You'd better install that whiteboard, you'd better encourage people to write on it, and you'd better hold those weekly Q&A sessions every single week. Likewise, if you're trying to create a friend boundary, I find it best to be direct. "It's been great seeing you so much lately. I'm going to be taking a little break now, though, as I focus on finishing my dissertation. I'll be in touch when things calm down." In your mind, you know exactly when things will calm down.

Hold Your Ground: It's something about human nature that a "don't touch" sign almost begs us to touch. We are fascinated with the word "don't" and want to test its limits. This will be the case with anyone who comes against your new boundaries, especially when they're new. But you must be strong. Don't give in now. You've done so much work to get to this point that you must hold your ground. Come up with a simple answer to nip complaints or questions in the bud: "I understand your concern, but this is what I need to do right now" works wonders.

Nonnegotiables: Wouldn't it be great if everyone always respected boundaries? But some boundaries require "No Trespassing" signs for a reason. Maybe there is a patch of really great blueberries on the other side, one thinks, only to find out after a broken ankle that the sign is there for a reason: There is a really dangerous ravine over the line, and the owner doesn't want others getting hurt. No Trespassing signs may not always make sense to others, but you still need to have them in place. Any boundaries you set should be nonnegotiable. You must believe in your mind that these boundaries are electrified. You can touch them, yes. But you will get a shock. Your system realizes, "Hey wait, this isn't actually totally *non*negotiable, there's a little wiggle-room . . ." and suddenly you've lost a wheel on your self-discipline car.

Now, a Note about Compromises: The world runs on compromises, so I can't leave them out here. Mastering the art of the compromise is a must for successfully navigating the self-discipline road. It's a must for navigating life in general. Remember, we are our own keepers, so we can compromise our boundaries without compromising everything else. It just takes an inordinate amount of strength to compromise once and not compromise the future. Make sure you desire the compromise (that it is in line with your values), and make sure it is worth it. Life is not perfect, we are not perfect, other people are not perfect. Compromises are the way we get around these things. We have to build bridges so we can accomplish things. Remember how I said there are many different building blocks and parts for self-discipline? Bridges are one of the most important features.

Compromises must be made according to your values. I cannot tell you what things to compromise on and what not to, because the list is different for everyone and even then, every situation is different. I will tell you, though, that there is always work to be done. Work will always be there. If not this work, then another work. But family? Family isn't always there. There are no other families waiting in the wings. As they say, "babies don't keep"—relationships don't, either. They need to be tended. So keep this in mind when you're faced with making a sacrifice or compromise.

Sacrifices: Sacrifices. There are two kinds to keep in mind when we discuss sacrifice and self-discipline. There's the sacrifice you make when it comes to work, and there's the sacrifice you make when it comes to life. You have to balance the two. Sacrifice can only come from one source, or you are left with nothing. If you sacrifice with both work and life, you end up with neither. Let me explain. Sacrifice is a dire-situation sort of thing. Sacrifice is not a daily occurrence—it can't be, or it isn't sacrifice anymore, it is the norm. Sacrifice means going above and beyond. It can mean giving when you thought you had nothing left. It can mean giving one thing up for another, or giving up a part of something precious to bring something else from good to great. Sacrifice involves a little bit of pain. A little bit of discomfort. It should, it has to; that's the point. Sacrifices must be uncomfortable. So, you can see that when you take (with pain) from both work and life, you are left with little. Sacrifices must be made with utmost care and attention. They are a self-discipline expert-level tool. You can sacrifice a paycheck for freelance freedom, but you have to make sure your life can survive it. You can sacrifice personal relationships for the sake of work, but you have to make sure you can survive it. You have to make sure you can live with the sacrifice. It can hurt, yes, but don't let it kill you.

BE YOUR OWN CHEERLEADER: YOU ARE AMAZING

....

Self-improvement is exhausting. And no one will be there at every mile marker with a glass of water and cheering signs to encourage you. That's your job, because you're your own keeper. But it's a fun part of your job.

This is probably my favorite part of the art of self-discipline because I am a celebrator of all things, big and small. New pencils? Hooray! New job? Even bigger hooray! It can be hard to find external cheerleaders these days, with everyone focused on their own self-improvement. They are out there, to be sure, but there is only one cheerleader you can know is always on your side. Yourself. Yay you!

For some reason, many of us don't like to champion ourselves. I think it's because of that humility thing we talked about, as if we think patting ourselves on the back undoes all of that good heart-work we've done to get humility on our side. Another lie. We are human beings and we thrive on rewards, accolades, words of appreciation, and other things that satisfy our need for approval. This can be a bad thing, but it isn't always. Let's take a look at cheerleading done the right way first, which will give us a window into how to cheerlead the wrong way.

Cheerleading Yourself Done Right

First off, you have to decide that you are worthy of a cheerleader. Tell yourself that you are worthy of rewards. Self-discipline does not negate celebration. If we really think about it, we might think that cheerleaders, celebration, and rewards are only for children and those who are weak with their self-discipline. These are lies. In fact, celebration is a friend of self-discipline. Cheerleading, celebration, and rewards keep the energy of self-discipline moving forward. Cheerleading promotes excitement, engagement, personal gratification, satisfaction, and acknowledgement. These are key parts of human existence, and it does not mean we are weak to seek them. It's practical, as well: Rewards help us complete the unsavory parts of self-discipline. No one loves the monthly spreadsheet-updating day we have to focus on at work. But having plans to go see the latest movie and get fro-yo with a friend afterwards makes it much more palatable.

We aren't accustomed to celebrating small things. But by capitalizing on the small things, and in essence making the small things bigger things, we're building encouraging motion and gathering creative capital. The little serotonin receptors in our brains get happy, and when they light up, the rest of us does, too. Get on board with self-discipline celebration. It's vital to the process.

Once you've accepted how awesome you are and that self-discipline loves celebration, you get to design your rewards. Since rewards are specifically designed by and for you, make sure they are something that truly motivates you. This is different for everyone. Perhaps a fancy coffee is reward enough for you, or maybe you want everyone on social media to know about your accomplishments. Maybe you actually want a little "YAY!" flag you can wave every time you do something amazing, or maybe just the act of crossing the item off your paper list with panache is cheer enough for you. Maybe you are eminently practical and want to reward yourself by letting yourself work on another work project that's more fun. You do you—just make sure it actually feels like a reward.

Set rewards for each mile of the race you're running. When you build rewards into your plan, you're suddenly a lot more likely to accomplish your goal. For instance, perhaps for every 20 pages you transcribe, you get to splurge on a new magazine to read on your break. Or maybe for every 10 new clients you get, you treat yourself to a manicure. Set goals along the way that match the difficulty of the task. No need to get a $40 manicure for making one tough phone call, c'mon now. Reward in proportion to the task and its results. Those are the rules.

You can even set bonus rewards, or "stretch" rewards, as the social fundraising platforms call them. When you go above and beyond your goals, and reach another, next-level goal, you get an even better reward. This might even be as big as a trip abroad, a financial investment such as an expensive business class, or some premium noise-cancelling headphones. When you accomplish a big goal, you get a big reward.

These rewards do not need to be work-related. The rewards can be related to personal life, and happen on personal time. See, work-related rewards (a new office chair . . . woo) are seldom motivating enough to keep us trucking along. Making at least some of the rewards personal ones brings a bit of accountability and excitement to the table.

Now, to be obvious for a minute: You have to actually accomplish something to get a reward. And you actually have to follow through with these rewards. So many of us say, "Yeah, yeah, I earned a manicure, great, I'll do it sometime later." *Some*time *later*. Later never happens. Sometime is not a time. Business guru Marie Forleo says, "It isn't real if it isn't planned." Your reward is useless unless it is on your calendar. Neglecting to fulfill your rewards is a terrible way to cheerlead yourself. It does absolutely nothing to revitalize your vital energy. That's all rewards are, really, a way to say, "I see you, vital energy, and I see your vital-ness and your crazy-awesome energy and I want to thank you for helping me accomplish this big task!" When we don't indulge in our reward, we let our vital energy down.

Rewards need not involve money, either. I mentioned the innate satisfaction that crossing an item off a list gives us. We are still hard-wired to like getting check marks in boxes, getting "satisfactory" on our report cards. Keep track of your progress by using a chart where you fill in x's, checks, or even heart or star stickers. Gone are the days of giant sticker charts of chores on our bedroom walls; welcome are the days of to-do checkboxes in our personal planners. If you're using my opening and closing procedures, reward yourself for accomplishing all of the opening/closing tasks each day for a week. Perhaps if you've juiced fresh juice all week at home, you can splurge on a $9 drink from your favorite juice bar on Friday.

Create rituals around your rewards. That's the thing. Make it a point to be disciplined and generous in your rewards when you are disciplined and generous in giving your best energy to your work. Create a cycle of positive reinforcement. Leave a little trail of breadcrumbs to the next reward so you know you have something to look forward to and are on your way. I am not a runner. I hate it. But if there is a cute little ice cream stand at the other end, I'll go for a run just about every night in the summer.

Sometimes we've reached a reward goal, and it's time to stop and get our reward (queue the Netflix!), but we're in a good groove and don't want to stop. How do we know if it is best to keep pushing through while we're in the mood, or if it's best to take a break and reward ourselves immediately? I prefer to ride the creativity wave first, then get my reward. I may even change the reward, since, perhaps after a great work session, I don't feel like Netflix-and-chill anymore but, rather, feel empowered and want to go for a walk. You can't "save" rewards, per se, and bank them up for later when you're feeling lazy. But you can change gears and reevaluate. You're the head cheerleader.

Crawl, Walk, Run: Be a Beginner

Being a beginner at something is the best way to channel your inner cheerleader. We all need to be oohhhed and ahhhed over for a little bit as we learn to crawl, and there's no harm in that. Encouragement does a beginner's heart good. If you haven't been a beginner at something lately, you're also missing out on a tremendous area of self-discipline growth. We all crawl before we walk, wobble a little when we learn to stand, flail around a little when we run at first. There are techniques to be honed, muscles to be toned, but all of that comes in time. Take your time.

I believe that part of cheerleading yourself means being kind to yourself in the beginning of the journey. We start new journeys every day, so we must constantly be kind to ourselves at beginnings. Beginnings are wonderful little things, all full of excitement and possibility. But there is fear, too, and a bit of a learning curve. We must be okay with the fact that crawling comes before walking, and walking before running.

Being a beginner is uncomfortable. If everything were easy, we'd all have black belts and bestselling novels and corner offices. But it's a good thing we don't all have all of those things. First of all, we all want different things, so we have to go after what we want. That means exploring and being a beginner. Second, if we haven't worked for something, chances are we won't be as careful with it. It's like a fast-food-meal toy versus our grandmother's beloved china doll. We have no investment, no history with the fast-food toy. It was quickly made, and quickly gotten. It will also be quickly destroyed or forgotten. The beloved family heirloom, though, has a history. It has earned its place on the top shelf, it has been loved and handled with care and respect.

We must go through the uncomfortable to get to the comfortable. There is no such thing as immediate comfort. Just like I said before about hot not being hot unless we have cold to compare it to, comfortable doesn't exist without uncomfortableness. When you're on the couch all day, it loses its loft and comfort. When you come home at the end of a long day, though, kick off your shoes and fall into its soft fluff, and you have indeed found comfort. Earned comfort. Unearned comfort? That's laziness.

And laziness makes my mind get all gritty inside. Do you know what I mean? Laziness makes me feel anxious-agitated-apathetic. It's what I call "gritty" and it's a terrible way to feel. It's also unpleasant to be around someone who feels this way. Laziness is detrimental to your health. Laziness brings on anxiety, agitation, and apathy. It's a fast track to burnout. Avoid laziness and grittiness at all costs. If your new job isn't going well, trust me, I know how tempting it is to give into laziness. I know how tempting it is to give up when your financial situation feels dire. When you lose the love of your life. I know what grittiness is and what laziness actually is because I have been there. I am calling it like I've seen it.

There are growing pains. There is no doubt about it. Improvement hurts a little. But muscles atrophy when they are not used, so there will be pain either way. I choose the pain of growth rather than the pain of battling atrophy. Being a better person, learning a new skill, getting used to a new job, adding a new habit to your routine: these are tough things. You have to stick with them through the growing pains. Improve your inner flexibility. How do you improve your inner flexibility? Here are some ideas.

Turn off Criticism: Criticism is rarely actually useful. Yes, often criticisms that come our way or that we direct at others are things we think are true. But truth does not always equal useful. Most of the time, criticism is just opinion. Like momma always said, don't give your opinion unless you're asked. Giving your opinion, i.e., your criticism, is almost never welcome, and it's simply a recipe for disaster. We have this convoluted term called "constructive criticism," which is just a way of sugarcoating what no one wants to hear. Having criticism stuck in your head makes it gritty. We have to actually turn. it. off.

Learn to Wield Your Weapons Wisely: We all have our sharp edges. They tend to show up the second things get hard or difficult. Maybe we think sharp edges help cut out uncomfortableness. Maybe we think if we show our claws, everyone else will back down, and we'll have "won" easily. Actually, those claws just end up cutting us and others. Personality's sharp edges do not actually improve situations. Ever. It is an act of self-discipline to learn to wield these weapons wisely. They might have their purpose, but the time and place for them are limited.

Remember Your Priorities: When you are centered in who you are and what is important to you, it's much easier to let the rest go. Chances are the things that are giving you grievances are molehills. Remember that we don't trip over molehills because we are self-disciplined. We don't make them into mountains, either. Center yourself over your priorities once again. This should help focus your perspective.

Delayed Gratification

Being a beginner is also an exercise in delayed gratification. We can see the end result (the black belt, the bestseller book, the corner office), but we aren't there yet. We have to work for it. Delayed gratification is an expert level tool in the self-discipline toolkit. You can only utilize it well when you've mastered other skills. The long-term reward system is difficult to implement from day one, because we simply get fatigued. Our willpower, our physical energy, our vital energy . . . we get drained before we can accomplish the task, which sets us back even further. Delayed gratification must be used in conjunction with cheerleading and the reward system to be worthwhile. We can keep perhaps one delayed gratification, pie-in-the-sky dream to work toward, but it cannot be our main focus point. We must focus on the pie here. We must be entirely invested in the regular-pie goals.

THE AFFLICTION OF ADDICTION: THE THIN LINE

....

Self-discipline easily becomes addiction. There, I said it. Didn't think I would go straight for the gut, did you? See, I've been there. I know the high that comes from constant accomplishment. The secret place that applause delights. I know where to find my reserve to get "just one more thing" done. Always just one more thing.

And I have crashed and burned because of those many, many "one" things. Anything can become an addiction. An addiction to anything, no matter how good the thing is in and of itself, is not a good thing. There is a very thin line between self-discipline and self-destruction.

Self-discipline is meant to be a good thing. A helpful thing to keep us on the right track, help us accomplish our goals, and to help us live the life we imagine. It is not meant to be a destructive thing. It shouldn't destroy us or those around us.

We can so easily let this quest of unattainable self-perfection ruin us. We become frenzied, maniacal almost, in our pursuit of perfection. No price is too high to pay, no cost too dear. Or so we think.

There is a price for perfection, and it is a steep one. Health. Health is always the price that is too high. The next-highest price is relationships. Relationships seem to go south instantly at the pressure of perfection. If you think there is no price to perfection, ask yourself this: when you give everything you have to achieve perfection, what is left? Nothing. Nothing to give to yourself, nothing to give to relationships, nothing to give to inner health and well-being. You cannot have it all.

Let me tell you something: self-perfection does not exist. We are born, we do life the very best we can, and then we die. We cannot perfect ourselves here on Earth. The pursuit of it merely breaks down the very vital energy that keeps us going. We slowly wilt, wither, and waste away, until our health has been compromised and we are victims of what we thought was perfection. Perfection eats away at us, literally. Did you know that anorexics' bodies literally start eating themselves? And it starts with the heart, because it is the hardest-working muscle. Trying to achieve "perfection" in the form of physical beauty causes your body to literally destroy your heart. You cannot have both: heart and perfection. And I choose heart. I choose health and relationships and having a life worth incorporating self-discipline into. Self-discipline is not the pursuit of perfection. Let me get that clear right now. This is not the handbook of perfection.

Once we admit to ourselves that perfection cannot be attained, we can free ourselves from the need to be addicted to self-discipline. Let me say it again: Self-discipline is not the pursuit of perfection. It is the pursuit of *better* . . . the pursuit of being the best stewards we can be of the gifts we are given.

It is about bringing self into center, finding purpose, and giving that purpose our all. The pursuit of progress with passion.

Don't worry about the two-steps-forward-one-step-back tango. This is life. We must dance with it. Sway with it, or you'll break some bones being dragged. No one likes that, so pick up your feet and move. Keep going. Even if you aren't quite on the rhythm, life rewards the movement. You've still made progress, so embrace it as part of the dance. My friend calls the "one step back" thing "life tuition." I like that. We give and take, we move and we sway and its life.

Social Media Addiction: Social media addiction is without a doubt an epidemic these days. We are attached to our phones for many wonderful reasons: documenting life, sharing with friends, connecting with family that live miles away. We are all busy, and social media allows us a quick way to connect. But we end up casting our connection net too far, it seems. We connect with strangers, and their lives and their friends and family. And we have to ask ourselves: Does it matter? Does it add to our lives? Or is it simply draining our resources? Our time and attention are two of our most valuable assets.

Screen Time: Screen time is a hip new term, particularly for parents. Children get certain amounts of "screen time" these days, and it is used as a reward or punishment: a babysitter, a teacher, and just about any other thing you want it to be. Screen time seems magical. Screen time is just as enticing to young brains as it is to old ones, if not more. Have you ever actually watched a child watch TV? They stare, eyes blank, little mouths open, chin and neck out, body stiff. Adults do it too, though a little less noticeably. I call it "turtle neck" from watching TV or staring at my screens too long. It's not attractive.

Time to purge: I don't recommend social media "fasts." When you come back, there's simply too much to catch up on, and you fall right back into the hole. What I do recommend, though, is a thorough and somewhat ruthless purge. Social media is your friend. Don't let it become a foe. You must continually prune your social media contacts, platforms, and interests to maintain a thriving social media ecosystem of your own. This puts some of the fun and excitement back in life too, by giving you options of things to explore when you have free time. You don't need to do it all, right now. Do it as time allows. Do it when the mood strikes. Do it when you need a stroke of inspiration. Cultivating your own social media ecosystem takes away the inevitable inadequacy we can feel when we see strangers' feeds all day, as well as the dreaded "Pinterest guilt" we are all so familiar with. There are many ways to do this, but here are a few ways to seek out the information instead of letting it come to you:

1. Unsubscribe from *all* email newsletters. Yes, *all*. Do not subscribe to any email newsletters at all. Worried you'll miss coupons? When you feel the shopping urge, search the internet for coupons. Better yet, install an app that automatically sifts through coupon codes for you on any website you're on. If you're going

shopping in the real world, do a quick search from your phone when you're in the store to download any available coupons. Only use coupons/apps when you need them. Similarly, keep a bookmarks folder of all business gurus whose emails you are deleting. When you have time to read a good article or two, open your bookmarks folder and find the one you want. Seek out the information when you need it, instead of being inundated by unnecessary information at all hours of the day (literally all hours; they send emails around the clock).

2. Put apps in grouped folders so you don't see alerts unless you go into the folder.

3. Unsubscribe from magazines and journals that pile up. Grab one from the newsstand when you have time to read it or a cover catches your eye (this makes airports especially fun; you can catch up on all of your favorite titles).

4. Cancel online subscription services. Online subscription services, such as *Sundance Now, Consumer Reports*, and other less-often-used services can be ditched. You won't feel the need to be constantly checking your accounts, and you'll save screen time.

Don't Let Social Media Relax You: Television doesn't relax us enough anymore, so now we have to have our phones in front of our faces *as* we watch TV. Talk about a short attention span! Check your social media in the already "in-between" times, such as when you're waiting in line at the grocery store or the doctor's office, when you're a few minutes early for a meeting, or when you are waiting for the laundry cycle to finish. Don't use any large chunk of valuable time, space, and energy for social media. Any large amount of time, space, and energy should only be used on tasks that either utilize or refill your vital energy tank. That is, be working or relaxing. Social media is a pseudorelaxing, just as television is—we invest our brains in something else for a while, but our souls don't get fed. Our souls don't feel soothed. We must refill our vital-energy banks when time is available, we must gather creative capital when we can, we must find an energy for our stress that is constructive. Social media is rarely constructive. I say this with many caveats, as social media is the way of the world now. It is how I let my grandma in Minnesota know how I'm doing halfway across the country. It's how I Skype with my nieces so I can see their loose teeth and their cupcake pajamas. It is valuable in those senses. And those things? Those things give back in equal measure. Scrolling mindlessly through the rabbit hole that is Tumblr, or Reddit, or Instagram . . . choose your poison . . . does not return in equal measure. It rots your brain like sugar rots your teeth—it feels sweet at first, but it has long-lasting effects.

The shortening of our attention spans that social media has cultivated is detrimental in many ways to cultivating self-discipline. It makes sense that self-discipline requires a strong attention span to get things accomplished and to focus in on the important things. Social media is like a chipmunk going to and fro, gathering acorns, getting its cheeks chock-full of them, and then forgetting where he stored them. It's a lot of work for very little reward.

How to Relax: Relaxing is an art form worthy of a book in and of itself. A wonderful art form it is, though, and a wonderfully personal one. The best part about relaxing is that you get to choose what relaxes you. Some might find a nighttime lake swim refreshing; for others, that is their definition of torture. You might love a weekend spent in the woodworking shop, while I want to be in the kitchen baking up a storm. For some, just the sight of their children or pets upon returning home is enough to lower their cortisol, while it sends it through the roof for others.

Learning how to relax can be tough. We have to settle into ourselves, which we aren't usually fond of doing in this fast-paced world. Shake your mind and anxiety out, shake your heart and body back into place . . . that's how you relax. I know, I know, you're still thinking, "But what does that *mean*?" Relaxation is an art, not a science, so I can only give you guidelines and have you try it yourself. Literally give your body a shake, thinking about letting go of anxious thoughts and calming your overactive body. Focus on slowing down your movements, letting your limbs be heavy as they are, and breathing deeply. Close your eyes. Think about your heart. Focus on it, visualize it, and keep breathing deeply. This is the feeling we try to capture when we're relaxing. It's happy, purposeful placement of our spirit, mind, and body. That means they are present and engaged in our bodies, but not chasing anything, be it thoughts or worries.

Most of us have many things that relax us, so we should keep cultivating a deep list (rather than wide) of things that relax us. A wide list is a lot of things that semirelax but are still engaging too many of the trigger points in our brains. A deep list reflects a deeply cultivated relationship with self that inspires multiple ways to truly relax in the truest of ways. We must turn off the negative, addictive parts of our brains to be able to fully relax and let go. Deep means of relaxation must come regularly. A once-a-year two-week vacation is great, but it won't keep you going the other fifty weeks of the year. For that, there are mornings, lunch breaks, evenings, and weekends.

Deep relaxation may be things like: a weekend getaway at the lake, camping, sitting by a fire reading all day, taking a midday nap, heading to a favorite café for a sweet treat and a bit of alone time, spending time lost in the celebrity gossip magazines you adore, playing a few rounds of golf, pumping iron at the gym, or practicing your hobby. Try kayaking, going to the library, taking an antiquing day trip, going to a museum, or spending the day at an amusement park. Adrenaline rushes are relaxing for some people. Crowds are no problem. For others, they need solitude and quiet for relaxation. Go with your gut instinct; if it calms your central nervous system and isn't dangerous or prone to adding to your addiction, it's fair game.

I also love a short list of relaxation ideas. These are instant-gratification things, the low-hanging fruit of relaxation that works without fault and is easy to attain. For me, iced coffee does it every time. A sip of a summer day. Dark chocolate is proven to release serotonin, our "happy hormone." Keep a stash in your desk for emergency situations. Run out to your car to spend ten minutes texting your family to keep in touch.

MY RELAXATION LIST

List your ideas for "deep relaxation" and "short relaxation."

_____

_____

_____

_____

_____

_____

_____

_____

_____

_____

_____

_____

_____

_____

_____

_____

_____

_____

_____

_____

_____

_____

_____

_____

_____

Make a cup of tea. Circle your neck and shoulders a handful of times. Here are some more specific ideas:

- Keep a rollerball filled with essential oil blended into a carrier oil in your desk, purse, or car for an instantaneous uplift. Uplifting essential oils include: peppermint, tangerine, grapefruit, lemongrass, and clary sage. Calming and comforting essential oils, such as geranium and lavender, are great, as well. Use five drops of lime and five drops of grapefruit in a 10ml rollerball, fill the rest with carrier oil, and roll onto your pulse points or simply smell from the bottle. (You can get an empty rollerball at most co-ops in the beauty supply section, or order them online. Use sweet almond oil for the best carrier oil.)
- Make an aromatherapy spray. Similar to the idea above, this diffuses aromatherapeutic essential oils into your environment. I like to use essential oils that promote mental clarity, since I find I am usually overwhelmed and exhausted when I need to relax. Fill a 4-ounce glass spray bottle with 50 drops of lemongrass essential oil and 50 drops of rosemary essential oil. Fill the rest with water. Shake before each use and spritz into the air. (Essential oils can eat through plastic rather quickly . . . they are very strong when concentrated, so be sure to use glass whenever possible.)
- Make a doctor's appointment you've been dreading, renew your library books, or tackle any other small-but-big task. You know, the tasks that are easy enough

to accomplish but take up way more mental space and anxiety than they should? For some reason, checking off a mental hurdle is hugely freeing and relaxing for most people, and it's worth it.

- Book something to look forward to. Be it a fishing re-treat, overnight stay, signing up for a class, trying out for a play—book something that refreshes your view of the future. Having something to look forward to—an endgame—helps you relax and focus.
- Send an email that excites you. Reach out to some-one for that long-shot gamble. Ask for something. Try something new. Introduce yourself. This is a great two-minute way to get some happy-work-vibes going, with nothing to lose.

Did you know you can relax anywhere and at any time? I mean it. Meditation, prayer, and deep breathing can happen anytime anywhere, and no one even has to know you're relaxing. You can do it in the car, at your desk, at a meeting.

Meditation: There are many different kinds of meditation. There are apps on your phone now with guided meditations. You can download meditations ranging from five minutes to a full hour, full of calming voices and reassurances, plenty of silence, and a few instructions for breathing and bringing awareness to your body. There are other tracks that do not feature words but only sounds, generally the calming sounds of nature—ocean waves, the forest ecosystem, or the combi-nation of water and land that exists in a lake landscape. Plug in those headphones. Let the silence, soft words, and gentle noises soothe you. Be well again.

Prayer: Prayer is a powerful tool for relaxation. I like to think of it as meditation with someone on the other line. Meditation is inwardly focused, but prayer is outwardly focused. Prayer gives the thoughts and feelings that are worrying us a place outside of us; we can hand them over. Meditation is wonderful for calming feelings, but it doesn't do anything with them other than tell them to be quiet and wait their turn. Prayer gives them to someone, in fact many times the only one, who can do something about them: God. There is no secret to talking to God; you simply talk to Him in your mind.

Breathing: You know I am a big fan of breathing exercises. They do so much good, mentally and physically. Breath is life, so we must keep our life well-centered and vibrant. A good friend once told me to "breathe into the pain," when something in your body physically hurts. Send your breath there because breath has healing properties. The same idea works with nonphysical ailments. Bring your breath attention to where your body is holding the tension.

KILL YOUR DARLINGS: IN LIFE AS IN FICTION

....

Killing your darlings is a frequently cited tenant of fiction writing, and writing in general. To kill one's darlings means to take the pieces of the book (words, sentences, characters, whole chunks of work) that you love too much, and to delete them, or literally kill them off (in fiction, remember). As writers, we become so enamored with our own work and our own characters that we often fail to see what the work as a whole needs.

It's the same as not being able to see the forest for the trees, and so many other good clichés. We get blinded by the investment in something and forget to take a look at the whole picture. We most certainly will not even be contemplating actually killing anything, we will be metaphorically slashing some parts of our life and work that we've become far too fond of.

Chances are, even reading two paragraphs into this chapter, you've got something in mind that is a darling you need to kill in your life. If not, I wish I could tell you what yours is, but it's different for everyone. But we all have our pet projects that are doing us more harm than good. What have you held onto for too long? What have you put too much of your vital energy into without a high enough return? What have you been overexerting yourself to accomplish, when it doesn't really matter that much in the scheme of things?

Examples of Darlings: *"Networking" groups that are really just friends meeting together, selling your wares at the local farmer's market every week even though you just barely break even, paying rent for an office space that you don't need because it makes you feel legitimate, being a member of a club because your mother-in-law wants you to, etc.*

Self-discipline requires all of our best efforts. We all have our projects that aren't worthy of our full attention. And so, we must kill them off. We must quit the committee we've been on for twenty years. We must quit staying up well past a decent hour to do our kid's school project because it ruins our productivity the whole next day. Yes, we must. These things do not serve us anymore, so we must stop serving them.

How to Say No to a Long-Time Darling: Good-byes are hard, there's no getting around it. A part of us stays with the project

MY DARLINGS

What things in your life do you need to let go of in order to grasp the more important things?

_____

_____

_____

_____

_____

_____

_____

_____

_____

_____

_____

_____

_____

_____

_____

_____

_____

_____

_____

_____

_____

_____

long after we've said good-bye. That's okay. In fact, that's good, because memories are just more creative capital. Here are some tried-and-true steps that will help you detach from a long-time darling.

Let your gut have its moment: Your gut will have something to say about this. Guts always want to be let in on decisions that involve the head and heart. Let it have its say. Chances are, it will tell you what I'm telling you, if you really listen: It's time to say no. But you do have to listen to it before it will relax enough to let you move forward. Take some time to get in tune with your gut. If you're not used to doing that, treat it like a relationship. Take yourself out to coffee. Relax your stomach. Breathe deeply into it. Let your mind sink into it. Then listen.

Determine to do it: If you haven't determined, with all of your self-discipline guts, that you will say no, you won't follow through. If you do manage to follow through, it will be a hot melting mess of back-and-forth regret-and-panic. This is likely to result in desperately returning to the project, making the breakup even worse. I wish I could tell you exactly how to do this, but it is different for every person and every situation. You simply must come to terms with the decision.

Make a plan: It may seem like a good idea to pick up the phone or type in all caps "I SAY NO" immediately when you make the decision, but this is not courteous. Remember, this has been a long-term relationship. It deserves respect as you separate. You enjoyed this project immensely; it has just outlived its purpose in your life. There's no shame in that—just about every-thing in our lives has an expiration date. Make a plan to separate. Will they need to find a replacement? Will you need to liquidate inventory? Do you have a contract you need to see through? Plan your exit to give everyone enough time to pivot.

Follow through: Once you've made the plan, you've sim-ply got to follow through. Be gentle but firm. Stick to your guns, with grace. Dig deep for your self-discipline here, as you may feel wobbly and unsteady as you let go of something that once took up time and energy. Instead of feeling the loss, fo-cus instead on where that time and energy can now go. If you don't have a specific use for the time and energy now, don't fret. Life has a way of filling time with good and unexpected things.

How to Say No in the Moment: Saying no in the moment may be even harder than killing a long-time darling. Saying no to a potential can be nerve-wracking for some of us. We fall in love with the idea of potential, and our self-discipline voice says, "Another project!" We love projects. We love hav-ing more things to be successful at. Just because we *can* do it, and do it well, doesn't mean we should. Here are a few things that self-discipline almost always says no to: "brain-picking" lunches with beginners (very different from a mentoring rela-tionship, which self-discipline loves), "networking" with the wrong clientele, any afterwork "work" event that isn't directly related to your goals, and basically anything else that seeks to take your vital energy with little compensation.

The actual saying no process is simple, once you get the hang of it. Try it a few times in the mirror or in a low-stakes situation first. Here's the script: "Thank you so much for thinking of me, but I won't be able to (fill in the blank). I hope the project goes well!" That's all you need to say. That's all you need to say for a major contract, a work event, or a kid's birthday party. This works in person, on email, via text, or as a voicemail. You don't need to offer any explanation. Train yourself to stop there. You don't need to add an apology ("I'm so sorry, but I won't be able to . . .") unless you actually mean it.

LAURELS ARE ITCHY: SO DON'T SIT ON THEM

....

Let's talk about our laurels for a bit. The wreaths of accomplishment perched on our heads proudly, for all to see. Our diplomas, our gold medals, our children's accomplishments, our personal achievements. These are exciting things, the stuff self-discipline thrives on.

I know you have, can, and will accomplish great things. How do I know you have accomplished great things already? Because you are you. Because you have gotten this far. Because I believe in you, and I know others do, too. I know that deep down, you have overcome obstacles inside you and accomplished things in your inner self that no one even gets to see. I give you laurels for those, my friend.

How do I know you can accomplish great things? You can accomplish great things because you are here, reading this book on self-discipline, wanting to do more. Wanting better things for yourself and more out of your life. That's a self-discipline win right there.

And how do I know you will? Because you have all the tools you need, all the heart motivation you can muster, and all the inner strength you can find. I know you will because science says if you eat a piece of fruit and then make a decision, chances are you'll make a good one. Stock up on fruit, because you're going to do amazing things. I can't wait to see.

When you accomplish great things, I want you to really relish them. Really take it in. Don't step on your laurel. Don't bow your head in humility and take your laurel off. Now I'm not saying you should swell with ego beyond the size of your head. Please don't do that; no one looks attractive with a swollen head. But they don't give laurels lightly in this world, you know. They don't sell knockoffs on street corners. You deserve this, you earned it. Acknowledge that. Acknowledge the work that got you to this podium. Let yourself feel the weight of it. Your discipline has paid off. Cry a few tears for the late nights and the muscling through I know it took to get you here. Then cry a few happy tears because you did it. You did it.

But each laurel has its time limit. Laurels are only shiny so long, only fragrant for a little while. Once they become dry and dated, they are crunchy, itchy, and absolutely terrible to sit on. How does this happen? It's just the way of the world. Every laurel anyone has ever achieved has dried up. This isn't to say a gold medal isn't still a gold medal. But after the Olympic cameras turn off and you put the gold medal in its case, you have to face life again. You have to do the postgold-medal life.

It's okay, because if laurels never went by, we'd never need to seek one out again, and we'd be stuck living in the past. Living in the past is a major foe of self-discipline. Forward motion, energy, vitality—these are the things we crave. The past

MY LAURELS

List your prized laurels from the past. Revel in them for one more moment. Then let them go and move on.

_____

_____

_____

_____

_____

_____

_____

_____

_____

_____

_____

_____

_____

_____

_____

_____

_____

_____

_____

_____

_____

_____

_____

does not hold any of these things. The past has a pull, though, no doubt about it. The past seems comfortable. We knew what we were doing in the past. And we won something because of it; so it must have worked! Our brains love security, our emotions love stability. We crave it. We crave the past because it is safe, and we are fearful. But self-discipline eschews safe and fearful. Self-discipline demands better of us. And we can do it, we can.

Sitting on our laurels seems comfy on the outside. A great accomplishment under our belts means we can take it easy for a while, right? Show off this shiny badge we've got while we slowly slip into laziness. I'm really not sure where and why this transition from having laurels on our heads to sitting on them comes into play. We need to nix this part of the narrative. We can put our laurels on a shelf to admire. We can put them behind glass or have them bronzed for posterity. But sitting on them should not be an option.

Yes, we *can* sit on them. But it isn't very self-disciplinary of us. It isn't being a very good steward of our best and most valuable assets. The world doesn't get to see our greatness. We don't get to see what we are capable of. Our vital energy goes stale and sour, our inner resolve can waste away in the face of perceived comfort.

I know you were worn out achieving your laurel. It was hard-earned and you deserve it. You're probably exhausted now. This is where we learn to rest, and not quit. Where we learn how to best refuel, instead of giving up.

The truth is, it is much harder to restart than it is to keep going. It takes much more vital energy to get going again than it does to keep going. Fits and starts, spurts and stalling out never accomplished much in the long run. When we stall out, we've lost momentum entirely. We have to start from scratch. We get rusty, we get water in the fuel lines, and that anxiety-laziness-depression spiral can begin. It happens to the best of us when we stall out. High-performance machines and well-oiled self-discipline machines have a little bit longer until it sets in, but it does.

The only way to combat this is to breathe, live, and work in the here and now. We cannot live or work in the past. We also cannot live or work in the future, no matter how hard we try. The past does not exist anymore. The future doesn't exist, either. The present is all we have, so it's all we can work on. It's all that deserves our precious vital energy. And trust me, there is enough work to do in the present. The past is a major foe of self-discipline. It loves to tell us lies. The past tells us we can never repeat history, we can never achieve another laurel or a better laurel. The past says, "You've peaked." The past says, "This was a fluke." The past says, "You'd better rest on this because it's all you've got and it's all you're getting." The past loves to portray a scarcity mentality. The past runs scared.

Yes, it is hard work to keep going after achieving a laurel. I get it. I graduated high school when I was 15. I went straight to college. I switched lives with another teenager for a week on a show called "Switched!" on ABC Family. A film crew filmed us for national television for a week. Here I thought I had this huge laurel, this exciting unique thing . . . everyone hated me. First off, I hadn't told very many people I was only 15, so the film crew made sure everyone knew. It was finals week and national film crews were covering campus. And add to that this 15-year-old freshman was the one getting all the attention. No one liked me after that. The school screened the airing of the TV show, and people booed. It was that bad. The rest of the semester was impossibly frustrating. I packed up my room with speed, said good-bye to hardly anyone, and went home to crash and burn. Everything that I was, and had earned, was on display on that television show, and it was booed, in front of all my peers. That sets a heart back. That pokes a hole right in the vital-energy reservoir.

Here's another truth about laurels: no matter how well earned and deserved they are, there will be some other people who will not like it. They might not cheerlead you. In fact, they might even boo you. Success threatens them. Everyone is a little insecure deep down, and we feel it when someone else gets something and we don't. It doesn't matter if we were first runner-up or we weren't even in the running—it matters that they have something shiny and we don't. We revert to being kids in a sandbox and throw grown-up temper tantrums. Do not let this damper your enthusiasm. It mustn't, because it isn't real. It's someone else wanting the same trophy you get for First Place simply for participating.

Other people just don't like the fact that someone else can manage the self-discipline they can't. I wish everyone who saw someone doing flat-out amazing things was inspired and did the same. But, in reality, we tend to tear those people down. We throw rotten tomatoes at them and hope they cool it on the amazingness. We don't want anyone to rise above the pack. The pack is fine, the pack is safe, the pack is where we can be a little bit lazy and not worry. In the pack, store-bought cookies are more than acceptable to bring to the neighborhood block party—no need to make layered palmiers from homemade puff pastry. A mediocre review at work is fine because your job still pays the bills. We think this twisted thought: If *I* can't make myself disciplined, *they* shouldn't be able to, either. Ouch, that's rough. It didn't read easily, did it? I hope not, because it is a lie, a flawed instinct. Our subconscious might feed it to us, but we need to spit. it. out. We somehow think their amazingness is making us look bad. It isn't. Don't worry. Besides, you can bask in their glow and get a little tan too, and learn from them. Shining people have something going on that's working, so stay close to them.

It's this strange phenomenon that sometimes we follow a big success with a big ol' flop. I think a lot of it is in our heads. A little bit of it could be the fact that we might have gotten booed, and who wants to willingly chase another booing session? We tend to get an internal feeling that we've "washed up" and there's no way we could compete with our previous accomplishment. This is only being mean to yourself. You wouldn't let a friend say that to you, would you? No, I sure hope not. Remember, creativity is a cycle and we have to peddle hard, so if you're feeling drained, just get back on the bicycle.

Pride tries to keep us safe. Pride wants to sit on the laurels, wants to protect us from future failure when we've already been successful. Punch pride in the face. There is no room for pride on the self-discipline journey. Remember, we talked about humility? Humility knows you can't sit on laurels. Humility knows it might be a little tough to get back on the creativity cycle after a big laurel comes our way. Humility knows that even if we flop around a bit after our big break, our big break still happened, and we are still light years ahead of where we were before. We are still making progress, and progress shuts pride right up.

THE FALSITY OF SCARCITY: JUST KNOW WHERE TO LOOK

....

I don't subscribe to the notion that we are all trying to grab a piece of the same pie. Guys, there are many, many different flavors of pie. The pie isn't scarce. Granted, the pie may be scarce in your cupboard, but the whole world has pie available, in every shape, form, and flavor. My favorite flavor pie is not your favorite flavor. Let me explain.

Differentiation is the key to success. You make your own flavor, add your own toppings, cut your own slices. Not only are there dozens of ways to make pie, there are dozens of ways to package pie, to eat pie, to showcase pie. Go crustless, braid the edge instead of flute it, make it savory instead of sweet, bake it square instead of circular.

If you can't make your own pie, buy the pie, and package it differently. Use every God-given gift, grace, and bit of grit you have to create your own version of the pie. This means every. single. person's version will be different. And if every single person has a different version, how can it be scarce after all? Do you see what I mean?

Scarcity is a lie in most creative cases. I do not mean to say that world hunger is a lie, or that the high numbers of people without safe or warm homes is a lie. I mean that creative capital is free to be had and that you are able to achieve something right now, using what you have. I guarantee it. Use what you have, what you can find, what you're given. Do the best you can now. Then reinvest, grow, gamble just enough, and you'll be successful.

I guarantee you have something. If you don't have money, maybe you "only" have time. Maybe you "only" have your words, maybe you "only" have your music, maybe you "only" have your own two hands. I put the word only in quotation marks on purpose. It is such a tenuous word to use there . . . only. No. You *have* time, words, music, hands. What a blessing. Now use them. You are you, and no one else is you, so that means that you are you-nique (couldn't help myself) and therefore you have something. It's just logic.

Sometimes we *are* faced with a scarcity challenge. Sometimes what we have looks pretty small, and what we need seems pretty big. These can be true circumstances, but it is only a circumstance. It is not the whole picture of reality. There is still pie. There will be more pie. There might not be a whole lot of pie on your plate right now, but don't despair.

What you possess is only yours to claim, and everything that has made you *you* pretty much negates the idea of scarcity, because everyone has a different role. Everyone has something different to offer. Don't put your beautiful hexagonal self in a square hole. It will bruise you up and it might even chip off a few of your magnificent characteristics. Hold out for something that fits. Hold on to the truth that scarcity is a challenge to overcome, not a reality.

Scarcity just means you have to do a little bit more work to find what's right. Don't give in. Don't settle. It isn't worth it in the long run, because crashing and burning won't be far behind. I absolutely know how difficult it is to be desperate and want to settle. Being desperate is a terrible feeling, and it drives us to destruction. Sometimes it's subtle destruction, and it doesn't look too bad at first. But most things built out of a negative feeling of desperation will not end positively. It's just the way the world works—desperation is not attractive. It does not attract good things.

Staring down the face of supposed scarcity requires confidence and strength of self. And oh, oh, does it require self-discipline. When faced with a scarcity situation, there are a few things you need to do.

1. *Take self-care seriously.* You absolutely must be hydrating, eating well, resting as much as you can, and doing gentle exercise. I know I say it a lot, but it really is foundational. Keep the foundation strong so you can build on it. If the foundation gets wonky, you're even worse off. Stay strong, hard as it is.
2. *Talk it out.* Things are tough. Emotions are running high, adrenaline and cortisol are fighting in your body over what you're feeling. You absolutely must not keep this in. Talk to friends, mentors, family, and your therapist.
3. *Focus on your strengths.* When you put the word out that you are facing a scarcity challenge and are looking for the next piece of pie, only focus on confidence. Discuss your strengths. Do not speak out of desperation and scarcity.

The scarcity is a symptom of the real problem; deal with the real problem and don't whine about the scarcity.

4. *Remember that confidence is rewarded.* The world rewards confidence. Relationships thrive on it, work goes infinitely better with it; you, deep in yourself, feel better about life. Confidence is rewarded; desperation is not.

If you truly feel you have nothing, I challenge you. I challenge you to help someone else who also has nothing. Help in any way you can, even if it's a hug or a smile. Help someone else, and it comes back to you. Build on it. Build relationship. Relationship is something. Smiles and hugs are something.

Start Somewhere: Somewhere is always better than nowhere. Something is always better than nothing. In fact, starting somewhere is the very best part because you get to see what you can do when the rubber hits the road. This is go-time, and that is exciting. I saw a news article on someone who had time, and he decided to spend his time offering to walk with people. Simply to walk alongside them. Walk them to work, walk with them to exercise, walk with them while they took their dogs to the park. He created a service that many of us secretly desired but weren't sure how to get: simple companionship. This cost him nothing. And it sparked something.

Reinvest: Take what you've discovered and implemented so far, and reinvest it in the future. I do not mean to "use" connections or people to your own ends, but rather to truly re-

invest. Invest more deeply. You can reinvest money, sure. If you earned $10, use $5 of it to buy something that helps make your business better. Ad time, business cards, etc. You can also reinvest time and communications. Time is precious so we must invest it wisely. Ask someone out for coffee. Really listen to their ideas for you, their concerns and their gifts. This is a precious exchange. They've given you their most valuable commodity, so be sure to reinvest that information, again, wisely. Keep the cycle going.

Grow Sustainably: When you keep the cycle going, wisely reinvesting your money, time, relationships, and communications, you'll be able to grow sustainably. You'll have a firm foundation and great floor joists and supporting rafters and excellent insulation. You can finish and furnish the space now. You can continue to grow with confidence. Your customers will be able to trust you, to know you are here for the long haul and that you grow with integrity and honesty.

Gamble Just Enough: While stability is the basis for building something well, a wild card of creativity is your ace in the hole. Gamble is a scary word in the world of self-discipline. Gambling is very shaky ground, very unstable territory. There are no clear paths, no guaranteed results, no success stories to emulate. Gambling is rogue, reckless, and most of all daring. Gambling can be *full* of that creativity that is vital to self-discipline success. The caveat is the "just enough." You must be smart and steady when making a gamble. How can you hedge your bets? Know that you can survive the worst-case-scenario situation. But also know that up-leveling anything requires a bit of upheaval. The results are worth it.

Change Things Up: Maybe you need more. Maybe you need to change to get pie. Mentally, emotionally, physically, or location-ally move. Pie doesn't come to us. Have you ever woken up with a pie on your front doorstep with the newspaper? Sounds nice, but me neither. We make pie. We choose ingredients, put them together, we spend time on it, we bake it. Or someone else does, and we give them money in exchange for their effort and the pie. So while pie does not just magically exist, it does exist. You just have to know where to look (and it's not on your front doorstep).

The people who believe in scarcity work with a scarcity mentality. This means they hoard things for themselves, unsure if they'll find more. That might manifest itself as them being overly protective of clients, job contracts, money, and anything that gives them emotional security. They might "use" people and things for their own advantage. They hold their cards close to their chest. People like this are touchy. You're bound to encounter them on your self-discipline road, but try not to become one. It's rather unbecoming. When you do encounter someone with a scarcity mentality, tread lightly. You need to treat them gently but with clear boundaries. Let them know that you deserve pie, too. That you are hungry, too. But also let them know that you are not there to take *all* the pie, or to take their pie. This can be a tough situation to navigate, and it might get a little messy.

Going even further than the scarcity mentality are those with a "no-pie" mentality. They don't believe the pie even exists. They've never smelled it or seen it, let alone had a piece to taste. These people are either apathetic or hungry. The apathetic crowd is the better of the two. These people might not care that they don't know what pie is. Pie is just another dessert to them, and they're fine with fruit. These are your fruit-for-dessert people. They go with the flow, don't rock the boat, are easy to work with because they aren't here for pie, they're just here to clock in and clock out.

Then, though, there are the hungry no-pie people. These people have heard *all* about the pie, and they want as much as they can get. These are the elbow-throwing, no-holds-barred people, and you want to stay out of their way. They are of no benefit to you or your self-discipline journey. In fact, they are only a detriment, a sure foe, so keep as far away from them as you can. Stay on your own path, seek your own pie, and don't associate with hungry no-pie people.

But who can help you along your self-discipline journey, particularly when you are facing a scarcity situation?

You are looking to spend your time with quality pie people. It doesn't matter if they've bought it or made it or scraped and borrowed to get the pie . . . if it is quality, you can bet they are worth sticking by. Keep your standards high for who you spend your time with, because it does affect your own mentality and your own self-discipline. "Bad company corrupts good character" is a familiar saying from the Bible (1 Corinthians 15:33), and it rings true. Your good character is worth more than anything you own, so when you face a scarcity challenge, rise to meet it, and bring good people alongside you.

CALM THE CHAOS AND CLEAR THE CLUTTER: CREATE CLARITY

....

A lot of times we claim scarcity because we don't have clarity. Clarity is key. Looking for something without clarity is like trying to find a needle in a haystack, except we're looking everywhere for the needle, not just in haystacks, and not just in one haystack in particular. Sometimes we're not even sure if we're looking for a sewing needle, a knitting needle, or a medical needle. Or is it a needle at all that we're looking for? You can see the problem.

We must calm the chaos and clear the clutter. Let's get back to clear vision, so we can accurately see our resources. Let's focus in on what matters, and what exactly we are looking for.

First, calm the chaos. It's tough to clear clutter from any area of your life, physically, mentally, spiritually, or emotionally, amidst chaos. Chaos comes from every angle—it loves to invade our space and make us feel inadequate and off our game. Chaos has *no* good self-discipline uses for us, and so it *must* go.

Chaos can be different for everyone. Think about what your interference is. What distracts you? What runs in your head on repeat? What pops in and out of your mind/office/life

CALM THE CHAOS

In the left column, list the things causing chaos in your life. In the right, list what you can do to calm the chaos.

Chaos	How to Calm It

and doesn't let you focus in? The physical things are the easiest. Your coworkers are constantly popping their heads over your cubicle. Your children aren't used to playing on their own and constantly want your attention. Your mother-in-law texts you incessantly, and it is driving you insane. The pets are always underfoot, and it's overwhelming.

Take an entire day and write down every little thing in your physical world that feels chaotic.

Then, make another column to the right of each item. This column is for brainstorming ideas to calm the chaos. This idea is based on Tim Ferriss's ideas on beating fear.[4] And what is fear? A whole lot of mental chaos.

Here's an example of what your list might look like:

Coworkers: Headphones, asking for a private office if the timing is right, working from home part of the workweek.

Children: Making small increments in individual play time each day, inviting friends over for playdates to keep them occupied, hiring a babysitter for a few hours a week.

Mother-in-law: This one is a bit tricky so your list might be different, but you'll have to broach the subject gently, either directly with your mother-in-law or through your husband, whichever works in your world.

---

4 Ferriss, Tim. "Why You Should Define Your Fears Instead of Your Goals." TED. https://www.ted.com/talks/tim_ferriss_why_you_should_define_your_fears_instead_of_your_goals.

Pets: Think about getting pet gates to keep the pets corralled in one area of the house. Make sure the pets are getting enough active time so they need rest. Keep children and pets separated so things don't get tangled up.

Brainstorm as many ideas as you can, to keep your options open. This also helps you realize there are solutions, and not just one, but probably many. Truth is, chances are you aren't the first one in the world to encounter this issue, so you can also ask friends for advice.

Next, choose and implement the top choice. This will take time. Your coworkers might not instantly get that headphones mean "I'm focused on my work." It might take a bit of time to train them, and you might need to actually say, "Oh, just a heads up, when I've got my headphones on, it means I'm really trying to get in the zone, so I'd appreciate it if we could talk later."

It is important that you really stick with the option you've chosen to implement and give it a try before moving on to the next one. It is too easy to simply say, "Nope, didn't work," to every option on the list and stay stuck in the chaos. Gird up your self-discipline and keep going.

Mental chaos is another monster altogether, but don't despair. It's one that self-discipline can tame, with time. The thing about mental chaos is that sometimes we don't realize it's happening. And sometimes we like it, because it keeps us busy. Sometimes we are scared of what might happen when we turn down the volume on the mental chaos. I hear all of these obstacles. But they are fears, all of them, and fear lies. Fear and worry will get you nowhere and will only zap your strength today. You need all of your vital energy, so tell fear to take a hike. Tim Ferriss talks about how to overcome fears using the Stoic theory of focusing only on what you can control and letting the rest go. The term Stoicism comes from the idea of sitting on a porch, or a stoa, and basically letting everything that is out of your control pass you by. Now don't go getting any ideas about sitting in a rocking chair worrying on this porch of calmness. Writer Erma Bombeck said, "Worry is like a rocking chair: it gives you something to do but never gets you anywhere." None of that, no. We reserve our strength for things that get us somewhere, for big moves we want to take, for things we can actually change.

We have to couple this idea of only working on things we can control with the idea of fear. Fear is controllable. But what we fear is not. See, we can decide whether or not we spend time fearing something. That is all we have control over. We must get rid of the fear and calm the mental chaos by focusing only on what we can control. This Stoic philosophy is self-discipline at its core—taking responsibility for what you can change, and making that change happen.

To turn off the mental chaos, you have to quiet fear. Most mental chaos is fear masquerading as something more important than it really is. Put fear in its place: a tiny place at the back of your mind where it cannot have a say. It doesn't get fed. It doesn't get let out for walks. Fear is a natural response that we need to keep in our lives, though, so we can't throw it out completely, which is why it still has its place, at the very back. Fear keeps us safe from danger and helps us know when it is time to get away. But our day-to-day fears are just fake situations we've created to feed fear. When you look at fear with reality glasses, it shrinks back down to its normal size.

Spiritual/emotional chaos is very similar to mental chaos, because a lot of it comes from fear. But where we can be a bit more logic with mental chaos, spiritual/emotional chaos doesn't like logic, as well. Here, we have to really listen to our hearts. Our hearts know a lot and are a great tool for self-discipline, because going against your heart simply fuels anxiety. When our hearts are fearful, we need to listen to them. Fearful hearts are a delicate thing. Everybody has some fear in their heart; it's part of being human. But when we are scared to unpack this fear, we become hard and unyielding, unable to express or experience emotions. Spiritual and emotional chaos is best treated by someone who can talk to you on a deeper level, such as a spiritual mentor, counselor, or therapist. It's hard to deal with heart matters on one's own, because they are shy and like to hide things from us. Someone who can ask the real questions about the fear is what we need.

Now let's talk about physical clutter: the stuff of life that can overwhelm us when it piles up. And pile up it does, despite our best intentions. We must constantly be taking out the trash. The real trash, and the extra trash of life, the things that we no longer need, that are no longer serving us or helping us grow. Get rid of physical clutter. Let go of things that no longer serve a purpose. If it brings up a bad memory, ditch it. If you're holding on to it out of fear of the future, let it go. Maybe the only reason you have something in your home is out of obligation to someone else: time to let go of both the item and the obligation. Be ruthless. Self-discipline requires a clean slate. Self-discipline requires clarity of space, as well.

I want you to get rid of three things right now. Literally right now. Put this book down (but don't put in the throwaway pile!) and go throw away or put in a bag to donate three things from your home or office. Phew, feels good, right? Keep going. You'll be amazed at the amount of clutter you have in your life that has no purpose and is only dragging you down. Then, you'll see fresh space and fresh perspective in its place. One caveat: once you've cleared the clutter, you have to actually get rid of it. Put it in the back of your car and go to the thrift store as soon as you're done. Don't let it hang around. Would you let the kitchen trash hang around in a corner? No. Same with life clutter trash. Then, clean everything. Give each surface a nice shine and glint. Get rid of spiderwebs and dust bunnies and water spots. Cleaning is good for the soul, both the process and the finished result. It says something deep inside us: things are new, there is room now, room to grow and room to expand with vital energy and creativeness and, yes, self-discipline.

Now that the clutter and chaos are gone, clarity is next. Clarity may come during the decluttering and cleaning process, or it may come separately. Sometimes we have to work a little bit for clarity. If it came easily, no one would be stressed, work would be great, families would be ideal, and we'd all have self-discipline certificates hanging on our walls. But clarity is earned. Clarity is given to those who seek it.

Your physical space should be clean, so find a comfortable corner and some alone time where you can seek clarity. Bring some tea or coffee, bring a notepad, bring some soft music, a plant . . . make a cozy little space that inspires you. Close your eyes and center yourself. Clear your mind. Get rid of any clutter that tries to make its way into your mind-space. Listen for the big story. Listen for the answer. Look for the answer in your mind's eye, but don't look in usual places. Don't look in spaces you know. Look in the blankness and see what pops up in front of you. Seek God, pray, meditate, find a comfortable mind space and sit there for a while. Sit there until you feel it. Clarity. It will come. Even if it doesn't come the first time, get in this space daily and seek it. Search it out, expect it to come, ask, and it will come.

And clarity, while it is a huge part of the battle, still doesn't do the work. Clarity is the map for getting to where you should go in life. For going where your deepest calling resides. But clarity still needs to hitch a ride on self-discipline.

CONCLUSION

·················

It doesn't seem so hard now, does it? Just kidding, self-discipline is always difficult. It just gets a little bit easier the more we do it, the stronger we become, and the more we invest in our process. Most people think self-discipline is all about forcing yourself out of sheer determination to accomplish things. But the harder heart-things that take work and effort will inform your self-discipline efforts and take them to new heights. Your curiosity will soar, your humility will help you engage with life on a deeper level, and having self-motivation is the quickest way to see follow-through. Clearing the clutter of your mental and physical space will help you make sure you keep molehills as molehills and that you don't fall into a scarcity mentality of having no pie. I want you to have the best piece of pie you can possibly imagine, topped with ice cream and sprinkles. And if the Pomodoro technique fails you, go for a walk. Breathe deeply, call a loved one, remember all of the good things in life. This sets our "self" at ease so we can focus on the "discipline" part of things again.

I hope this book has helped you find some clarity from the life-chaos that so often gets in the way when we try to walk in self-discipline. Disciplining oneself to do what's right despite the temptation to do what is easier . . . oh, that is a battle against spirit and flesh and blood. We do not battle our self-discipline foes in vain, though. Those laurels are worth achieving, because the world should hear about what's setting your heart on fire. And even if you have to be your own cheerleader most of the time, remember, I'm here, and I'm cheering you on.

NOTES